PLANNING
for LEARNING

Collaborative Approaches
to Lesson Design and Review

PLANNING
for LEARNING

Collaborative Approaches to Lesson Design and Review

Mary Renck Jalongo
Sue A. Rieg and Valeri R. Helterbran

Teachers College, Columbia University
New York and London

Published by Teachers College Press, 1234 Amsterdam Avenue, New York, NY
10027

Library of Congress Cataloging-in-Publication Data

Jalongo, Mary Renck.
    Planning for learning : collaborative approaches to lesson design and
  review / Mary Renck Jalongo, Sue A. Rieg and Valeri R. Helterbran.
      p. cm.
  Includes bibliographical references and index.
  ISBN: 978-0-8077-4736-0 (pbk. : alk. paper)
  ISBN: 978-0-8077-4737-7 (cloth : alk. paper)
      1. Lesson planning. 2. Group work in education.   I. Rieg, Sue A.
  II. Helterbran, Valeri R. III. Title.
  LB1027.4.J35 2007
  371.3028--dc22   2006022574

ISBN: 978-0-8077-4736-0 (paper)
ISBN: 978-0-8077-4737-7 (cloth)

Printed on acid-free paper
Manufactured in the United States of America

14 13 12 11 10 09 08 07   8 7 6 5 4 3 2 1

Contents

Acknowledgments

Several teacher educators, preservice teachers, inservice teachers, and school administrators contributed to this book.

The cases of teacher educators Larry Tinnerman and Jim Preston appear in Chapter 4 and Chapter 5, respectively. Jim Preston also contributed the lesson plan in Figure 1.2. Qiuyun Lin and Larry Tinnerman collaborated to compile the annotated list of websites on lesson planning in the Appendix.

Preservice teachers Jenica Harshbarger, Carrie Long, and Kelly Livingston—all students of Natalie K. Conrad from the University of Pittsburgh at Johnstown—allowed us to use their dialogue on the collaborative planning process in Chapter 3. Mary Landis, Greg Meyer, Autumn Calnon, Rebecca Lutes, and Erin Blank, all undergraduate students of Sue Rieg, provided comments about their experiences with collaborative planning in Chapter 3. Jim Preston's students at LaRoche College—Bruce A. Allen III, Linda R. Cessar, Colleen Gonzales, Shannon Sandberg, and Margaret Tynes—each supplied written comments for the case in Chapter 5.

Practicing schoolteachers and former Master of Education students Doug Anke, Samantha Isaac, and Katie Britton contributed their thoughts and experiences to this work as well. In addition, a group of practicing teachers participating in a history education grant graciously agreed to allow us to use their (anonymous) survey comments: Molly Weber, Donald Halin, Arlene Novels, Kristine Bunyak, Joe Girardi, Michael Rieg, Mary Kay Rura, Loletta Rupe, Edward Kocinski, Julianne Laird, Donna Sabbia, Linda Cribbs, Peggy Garbrick, Susan Kovalcik, Lori Laverick, Katie Bungo, Janet Murtha, Lana Buchanan, Laura Irvin, Susan Stitt, and Robert Rado.

Administrators with a commitment to collaborative planning also made a contribution to the book. Sharon Porterfield, a public school administrator with Armstrong Area School District and doctoral program graduate, agreed to be interviewed and quoted, while administrators Roberta Kuhns and Rod Bisi of Derry Area School District permitted us to observe their district-wide collaborative planning process.

We thank all of these educators for their insights and willingness to participate in our book project. Their words and experiences brought the precepts of collaborative planning to life by showing, rather than telling, how planning together affects the teaching/learning process.

Introduction

WHILE VISITING FRIENDS in Florida I met a married couple who had left careers as high school teachers to start their own housecleaning business. They cheerfully enumerated the advantages of their new job: flexible hours, more time spent together, greater physical fitness, less stress, good salaries/tips, and vacations that were not dictated by the school calendar. True, the couple admitted, they had lost some social status and were no longer working in the profession in which they had invested 4 years of college study. Yet some of the sources of satisfaction that had eluded them as teachers were accessible to them for the first time. They mentioned such things as the ability to exercise a high level of control over their work and resources, the freedom to select an efficient system of operation, and the luxury of sticking with it. Perhaps most gratifying of all, they now left work behind at the end of the day. Reactions from the pair's former teaching colleagues varied considerably, ranging from those who thought they had lost their minds to those who envied them.

If new teacher attrition rates are any indication, the perceived drawbacks to classroom teaching implicit in this story are not unique. Approximately one-third of new teachers leave the profession within 5 years, while teacher turnover is 50% or higher in schools in low-income communities and higher still for teachers with emergency certificates (Darling-Hammond, 2003a; Ingersoll, 2001). Teaching can be characterized by complexity, unpredictability, and incessant calls for reform to the point where the downside can overshadow everything else. One novice teacher in an urban first grade captured the inevitable ups and downs of a teacher's existence when he said, "Some days I feel like I could teach the world, and other days, I wonder how I ever allowed myself to get into this mess we call public school." Evidently, he is not alone in experiencing such frustrations.

> Every urban school district in America, it seems, is struggling to improve
> student achievement, and every politician, it seems, has a solution. Improv-
> ing teacher training, reducing class size, lengthening school days, testing
> students, and tying teachers' salaries to test scores are just a few proposals.
> . . . The result? Teachers continue to work in isolation from one another, and
> administrators remain disconnected from what goes on in the classroom.
> In addition, adversarial relations between teacher unions and administra-
> tors continue to thwart most serious attempts to improve what goes on in
> schools. (Wilms, 2003, p. 606)

Some educators have resigned themselves to becoming mindless functionaries who teach to the test and feign allegiance to whatever quick fix for schools that is being promulgated all around. Facile answers fail to recognize that higher expectations for student learning necessitate a concomitant effort to enrich and enlarge opportunities for teacher learning. If the history of education has taught us anything at all, it is that no significant, enduring improvements are made unless teacher expertise is enhanced in the process. Why is this so difficult to accept? No one is so foolish as to think that the field of sports medicine will advance without better doctors or physical therapists. No one expects to prevent terrorism at airports or post offices without training the workers about new security measures. In virtually every walk of life other than education, it is assumed that it is well worth the time and money invested to improve the workforce. Yet when it comes to improving education, there is insistence from politicians, the general public, and the popular media that better schools can be achieved by public outcry, standardized tests, or edict turned legislation.

This book argues, against fashion, that a single-minded focus on raising students' test scores not only fails as a solution, but is part of the problem. Teachers who work with limited resources, have few opportunities for colleagueship, and lack administrative and community support for their efforts may begin their careers with bright hopes. But expertise withers and wanes in environments inimical to professional growth. Education is a world where measures of success are once removed—determined not by what teachers do but by the effects of teachers' behavior on student learning. When teachers are limited, their limitations have profound consequences for students. Society may manufacture a new surface layer for schools; however, when the subfloor is not sound, the flaws beneath will telegraph through. What makes education even more perplexing and deceptive is that underlying problems are not immediately apparent. Only time will reveal the flawed underlayment of shortsighted solutions as damage up at the surface; poor installation of an innovation becomes visible with wear.

We undertook this book project because planning is the point of contact, the interface of theory, research, and practice. If, as Jerome Bruner argues in *The Culture of Education* (1997), the challenge of our era is to achieve a meeting of the minds, then collaborative planning holds the greatest promise for connecting teachers' goals with students' conceptual understanding, for bringing novice and expert educators together, and for linking basic and higher education. We began this project with an admiration for the collaborative teacher planning processes that are integral to Japanese lesson study, as described and analyzed by U.S. writers (LeTendre, 2002).

> [Lesson review] is a simple idea. Teachers collaboratively plan a lesson that is taught by one group member while others observe and carefully collect data on student learning and behavior. The student data are then used to reflect on the lesson and revise it as needed. Lesson study is a teacher-led process in which teachers collaboratively identify a concept that is persistently difficult for students, study the best available curriculum materials in order to rethink their teaching of this topic, and plan and teach one or more "research lessons" that enable them to see student reactions to their redesigned unit. Ideally, a lesson study group allows teachers to share their expertise and knowledge, as well as questions related to both teaching and subject matter. Lesson study groups may also draw on knowledgeable outsiders as resources for content knowledge, group facilitation, and so on. (Ashby, Lee, & Shemilt, 2005, p. 80)

As the book evolved, it took a somewhat different direction that focused more broadly on a reexamination of lesson design and planning. This may have occurred because, as an author team, we admit to being unusually practical in our outlook. We spend our days teaching preservice educators how to write lesson plans, supervising student teachers, working with in-service teachers in graduate classes, and preparing the next generation of teacher educators. As former public school teachers and principals, it was difficult for us to imagine a U.S. school that would lavish a year or more of work on a single lesson, as is common practice in Japan (Fernandez & Chokshi, 2002; Watanabe, 2002). What emerged from delving into teacher planning was unsettling. Although lesson planning is considered to be important, it is our considered opinion that not much has changed where lesson planning in the United States is concerned since our days as undergraduates. Granted, there is a bit more emphasis today on reflection and academic standards, but there is very little that represents a major stride forward in the link between teachers' planning and students' conceptual understanding. Interestingly, we discovered that we have like-minded colleagues in countries throughout the world, colleagues who are striving to make planning the centerpiece of professional development. Although the terminology might differ—teacher professional growth plans in Canada (Fenwick, 2004), building network contacts in Finland (Kärräinen, 2000), or professional development for outcomes-based education curriculum development in post-apartheid South Africa (Onwu & Mogari, 2004)—the focus was consistent. In every case, lesson design and planning were completed in the company of peers and had taken on an importance once reserved for in-class instruction alone. We emerged from the other side of the five chapters of this book as staunch advocates of collaborative lesson planning.

CONTRIBUTIONS OF COLLABORATIVE LESSON PLANNING

The assertion that the lowly lesson plan could make an important contribution to education may seem counterintuitive or outlandish at first. The lesson plan is about as surprising to educators as water is to fish; novices flail about trying to discover the plan's mysteries, expert teachers seem to glide through, and teacher educators are inundated with plans produced by college students in teaching methods courses. The sort of planning discussed in this book is very different from these lesson plans, which exist in abundance. Far from being a dreary exercise in following directions, the lesson is "a complex, dynamic system. Its analysis reveals connections and generates new insights, likely to improve the whole educational process" (Penso & Shoham, 2003, p. 326).

When a lesson plan is developed and analyzed in collaboration with peers and colleagues, its power to influence teaching is intensified. In the process of such collaborative planning, teachers achieve important professional development goals, such as:

- Establishing mutual trust and respect in order to function as responsible colleagues capable of giving and accepting criticism (Eaker, Dufour, & Burnett, 2002).
- Agreeing upon worthwhile teaching goals and putting forth a concerted effort to improve students' learning (Fernandez, Cannon, & Chokshi, 2003; Gagnon, Collay, Dunlap & Enloe, 1998).
- Engaging in an in-depth analysis of the learners' responses and work products that is translated into more effective teaching (Putnam & Borko, 2000; Sweeney, 2003).
- Meeting regularly and engaging in a cycle of planning, teaching, examining results, revising, and reteaching until the result is

exemplary lessons that contribute to the professional knowledge base (Curcio, 2002; Lewis, 2000, 2002; Stigler & Hiebert, 1999).

Collaborative planning has the power to change schools for the better where other innovations have failed or faltered because it addresses two persistent and difficult issues in the field of education. First is the gap between research and practice. Collaborative teacher planning deals with this age-old division by blurring the boundaries. The words *research* and *expert* are no longer the exclusive province of university faculty as classroom teachers participate in a form of action research with practical consequences: collaborative lesson design, planning, and evaluation.

A second perennial problem in education has to do with how the field handles innovation. There is a constant clamor for change, and education has a well-deserved reputation for pendulum swings rather than steady, incremental advances. Collaborative planning holds promise as a response to innovation because it represents a synthesis of so many enlightened educational ideas: reflective practice (Schon, 1983; Zeichner & Liston, 1996), expanding teachers' repertoires (Joyce & Calhoun, 1996; Wasley, 1999), teacher research (Cochran-Smith & Lytle, 2002; Sweeney, 2003; Wideen, Mayer-Smith, & Moon, 1998), induction programs for new teachers (Feiman-Nemser, 2003), and teachers as curriculum developers (Adams, 2000b), to name a few. The best that each of these initiatives has to offer is subsumed in high-quality collaborative planning processes. Reflection is enriched by multiple perspectives on the shared object of the written plan and peer observations of those plans put into action. Teachers engage in research that has relevance for the particular contexts in which they work, and lessons are valued for their power to support students in attaining greater knowledge, skills, and understanding of material that matters. Like a magnifying glass that concentrates the full spectrum of light to generate heat on a sheet of paper, collaborative planning gathers together the power of a spectrum of educational ideas and concentrates their energy on a single, highly effective lesson.

CHALLENGES TO COLLABORATIVE PLANNING

For all of its potential benefits, collaborative planning is not without its challenges. The media and political rhetoric routinely portray teachers as uninformed, self-serving malingerers who need to be whipped into shape through tough talk and even tougher tests. In this climate, learning to trust teachers enough to give them the time and opportunity to plan is a major obstacle.

A 15-minute planning period or a 30-minute department meeting will not suffice, and the work of Snow, Griffin, and Burns (2005) offers insight into the resistance that might come from the teachers themselves when collaborative planning is proposed. In their analysis of the research, they argue that teacher preparation is "a developmental process of progressive differentiation emerging from recurring cycles of learning, enactment, assessment, and reflection" (p. x).

Marginal teachers may regard such forays into group planning as an ego threat that will expose their ignorance. Even teachers with established expertise, if they live in a school culture that emphasizes extrinsic rewards, might fail to see any benefit to sharing their recognized and established expertise. After all, many master teachers in the United States have, through sheer dint of effort, learned to "survive elegantly" in the bureaucratic organization we call school (Kraus, 1984). Thus, whether the teachers are highly skilled or barely skilled, resistance is a predictable initial reaction. Such a reaction is compounded by school cultures that emphasize carrots and sticks. Making the transition to collaboration will take time to build trust, respect, and the confidence that the work emanating from the group will be, above all, directly applicable to the daily concerns of classroom teachers. Generally speaking, those concerns include strategies for adapting instruction to meet the needs of diverse learners, pedagogical approaches that make subject-matter knowledge accessible to all students, meaningful connections between academic standards and curriculum, and the formative and summative assessment of student attainment of learning objectives (Darling-Hammond & Bransford, 2005; Snow, Griffin, & Burns, 2005).

Perhaps the biggest challenge to effective collaborative planning is the difficulty many teachers face in trying to move beyond the routine, behavioral, one-size-fits-all approaches. For example, when college instructors urged preservice teachers to move beyond behavioral approaches, only 1.2% of the 2,416 social studies lesson plans produced reflected a departure from routine teaching (Zeegers, 2000).

Another obstacle is lack of patience and persistence in a society that celebrates the sound bite. Collaborative planning addresses school improvement at the instructional level. As such, it requires a major readjustment in approaches to educational reform. For generations, the unit of improvement in education has been the nation, the state, the district, or the school. Collaborative planning improves teaching from the inside out, by beginning with small groups of teachers who share a goal and then extending the successes of that planning to other classrooms, schools, districts, and beyond.

An additional challenge is the taken-for-granted teacher isolation that characterizes many U.S. schools. Just as city dwellers can feel lonely in a throng, teachers can continue to feel isolated in faculty meetings. The typical meetings at typical schools are little more than announcements read aloud, managerial items for discussion, or a presentation by a visiting expert. Teachers in the United States have been immersed in "fictions of teamwork" (Sennett, 1998) that reward superficial signs of unanimity rather than the productive friction of genuine colleagueship (Jalongo, 2002). If collaborative planning is to fulfill its promise, teachers will need models of support and exemplars of practice that take the culture of U.S. schools into account.

RESEARCH ON LESSON PLANNING

It has been 2 decades since the latest wave of research and writing about lesson plans was produced. Clark and Peterson (1986) characterized these studies to be of two basic types. The first category took a cognitive psychology approach and examined planning as a set of mental processes that required teachers to visualize the future, take stock of means and ends, and establish a framework to guide future action. In the second group of studies, teachers became key informants or collaborators in qualitative studies that examined what teachers do when they say they are planning. A major finding of both types of studies was that becoming an expert teacher demands thoughtfulness (Clark, 1996; Meier, 2002). As we will demonstrate in this book, collaborative planning processes broaden the scope and impact of teacher thoughtfulness by applying it directly to the improvement of learning for students, colleagues, and the profession. Just as the Internet was a networked response to the information explosion, networks of teachers are a timely and appropriate response to the curriculum explosion that covers more and aims higher. Collaborative planning processes harness the power of thoughtfulness by connecting it to instructional strategizing in the company of peers.

In order to build our argument for collaborative planning, we deliberately weave together the literature on lesson planning in the United States and in other countries. In addition, we have plaited together strands of research on the professional development of preservice and inservice teachers, theories of cognitive psychology—particularly those that examine expertise and wisdom—along with our personal/professional experiences with classroom teachers, both those enrolled in university classes and those working to improve teaching at their respective schools.

ORGANIZATION OF THE BOOK

Chapter 1 begins with a critique of the traditional lesson plan. The premise of the chapter is that, based on a review of the research on lesson planning, the limitations of linear plans outweigh their advantages. Chapter 1 also describes how collaborative planning was used in a college classroom to create a community of learners and take some tentative steps toward changing experienced teachers' ideas about the role and function of lesson planning.

Chapter 2 begins by developing a rationale for the reflective planning processes that serve teachers well throughout their professional careers. It is a candid discussion about the obstacles to planning with colleagues and ways to counteract them, and includes several practical illustrations of collaborative planning processes in action.

Chapter 3 discusses the role of collaborative planning in teacher preparation and initial licensure programs. One of the challenges in working with preservice teachers is to persuade them that thorough and thoughtful planning is the best response to the host of concerns they have about their personal ability to fulfill the professional role of teacher. Accounts of new teachers' experiences often center on a clash between idealistic expectations for teaching and the realities of daily life in classrooms ensconced in bureaucratic organizations. Chapter 3 argues that new teachers need to develop the ability to think on their feet, assess a wide range of situations, engage in ethical reasoning, study the consequences of their decisions and pedagogy, and put their insights to use in informing their planning and practice (Ball & Cohen, 1999). We contend that collaborative planning offers the kind and amount of support that novices need in order to persist despite the often overwhelming demands and challenges they confront as relative newcomers to the profession.

Planning plays a very different, yet equally significant, role in the lives of experienced educators. Most depictions of experienced teachers emphasize their need for renewal (or to use Erik Erikson's [1993] term, *generativity*) and their desire to contribute to the professional development of their less experienced colleagues. Chapter 4 presents the perspective that collaborative planning processes can support veteran teachers' need to be refreshed and to expand their sphere of influence to the next generation of teachers, professional colleagues, and the field of education.

Chapter 5 addresses the call for evidence of effective teaching. Consistent with the book's thesis, Chapter 5 will show how collaborative planning can result in the very types of artifacts that document exemplary outcomes in schools and postsecondary institutions.

Planning for Learning: Collaborative Approaches to Lesson Design and Review calls upon educators at all levels to reconsider widely accepted and familiar approaches to lesson planning that are incapable of measuring up to the nation's ever-escalating expectations for student learning and teacher performance. In the pages that follow, we reject the unexamined plan, urge teachers to revise and reteach on the basis of student response data, and elevate the lesson plan to a collaboratively negotiated curricular object that possesses the power to change the culture of schools.

—Mary Renck Jalongo
Indiana, Pennsylvania
March 20, 2006

CHAPTER 1

Reexamining Lesson Design and Planning

A student teacher in a fourth-grade classroom is teaching a lesson on the mass media. In haste she seizes upon an activity (recalled from her days in middle school) in which children locate examples of propaganda in newspapers and magazines. Early the next morning, the student teacher arrives at school without the resources that are necessary to complete the activity. She spends the first 30 minutes of her day racing from classroom to classroom in search of magazines or newspapers; unfortunately, not much is available. When her lesson begins at 9:00 a.m., the student teacher places the paltry collection in the center of the table and announces that there will not be enough materials to go around. With that, some children deftly slide materials closer to them, and others object loudly. She tries to stop the bickering with, "Okay, does everybody want to get into groups or something?" and 28 fourth graders launch into a frantic effort to connect with friends and avoid being left out. The student teacher rescinds her earlier instructions and states that she now will assign students to groups, amid cries of protest. As she pauses to assemble scissors, paper, and glue, three students whisper their plans to circulate a petition against the student teacher's unfair practices.

EXPERIENCED EDUCATORS may wince at the multiple procedural errors in a lesson that this beginner described as a "disaster." Most teachers could recommend several steps that would have made the lesson more successful; the student teacher cannot. She attributes the failed lesson to her fourth graders' reputation for being unruly and her inexperience with classroom discipline. This newcomer assumes that, with additional practice, all will be well. Yet unless she learns to plan effectively and profit from her mistakes, her life as a teacher will consist of first-year struggles repeated over and over again with new groups of students. In her search for solutions, she has rejected thoughtful planning.

CONFLICTING PERSPECTIVES ON LESSON PLANS

What was (or should be) the role of the lesson plan? The lesson plan as it is operationally defined in most colleges of education consists of an introduction, objectives (behavioral or not), materials, procedures, and evaluation, all produced by an individual teacher candidate or classroom teacher. The typical lesson plan would portray the act of teaching as a linear sequence of events directed by the teacher and linked to prespecified objectives. Most teacher educators are well acquainted with the traditional lesson plan. The authors' institution, for example, requires this structure and offers the guidelines shown in Figure 1.1.

Some teacher educators might argue that a plan that conformed to this structure would have been a "life saver" for the student teacher in the opening scenario. Lesson-plan purists contend that clear guidelines and consistent formats are a tried-and-true route to effective instruction. Yet the lesson plan—at least as most teacher educator traditionalists understand it—approaches myth. Cornbleth (1987) defines myth as a widely held belief with tenuous connections to pertinent evidence that is "an integral, often unexamined part of our contemporary culture, including our professional discourse in teacher education and teaching" (p. 187). Surely the everyday lesson plan qualifies as a myth in education because there is no empirically derived lesson plan format that captures what exemplary teachers do in the classroom (Kagan & Tippins, 1992). Even devotees of the detailed, linear lesson plan are forced to concede that plans must be adapted, adjusted, or even abandoned at times. Transforming an acceptable written plan into a successfully taught lesson is no small hurdle for

---

Figure 1.1 The Traditional Lesson-Plan Format

I.   **Heading.** Lesson number and title, your name, date lesson is to be taught, discipline(s), grade level, number of students, and allocated instructional time.

II.   **Rationale & Background.** Address lesson purpose, justify why students should experience this lesson, specify alignment of this lesson with standards, and explain how students can "connect" to the lesson based upon prior knowledge or experiences.

III. **Objectives.** Lesson objectives represent specific and intended learning. If goals represent the "destination" in terms of the unit, you might think of objectives as the various routes you take to reach that destination. Objectives include an "action verb" that speaks to that which you as the teacher can measure and/or observe. For each objective, you also must clarify the PI (Performance Indicator) that will enable students to demonstrate the learning and you, as the teacher, to monitor and assess the learning.

IV.   **Resources & Materials.** Specify the resources and materials needed in the lesson delivery and required for students to complete activities.

V.   **Concepts.** If students remember nothing else from your lesson, what is the most important generalization you would want them to understand, grasp, or formulate? What is the underlying premise that makes this lesson important for students to experience?

VI.   **Procedures**

A.   *Introduction & Motivation.* Describe your introduction with the following elements evident: engagement of all students, communication of intended learning in language understood by learners (objective), and connection of the lesson to prior learning and/or experiences of the students. Remember the purpose of an introduction is have all students engaged and focused on the learning that is the basis for the lesson and to do so expediently so that time needed for the lesson body and closure may be maximized.

B.   *Lesson Body.* Describe the lesson flow and what teacher actions facilitate the development of the lesson and student learning. Lesson body should indicate key questions you may want to pose to generate student discussion or check student understanding. Also, describe student actions in terms of activities in which they will be engaged. Again, ensure that there is alignment of teacher and student actions to the objective(s). Through the development of your lesson body, indicate appropriate adaptations evidencing differentiation of instruction based upon student need.

C.   *Closure.* Lesson closure provides students with an opportunity to reflect and summarize their learning. Aligned with objectives, through closure, students have an opportunity to demonstrate one or a combination of the following: process learning beyond the knowledge/comprehension level, review main concepts/key points of lesson, and/or reflect upon their learning in relationship to the objectives.

VII. **Evaluation.** This section of your lesson plan addresses two aspects of evaluation: assessment of student learning and your assessment of the lesson.

A.   *Student Assessment.* Briefly describe the various means you used to assess student learning and specify the evidence you have to determine whether students learned. In other words, how do you know what students learned as a result of that lesson? Based upon student responses to the lesson, what potential modifications do you need to make in the next lesson?

B.   *Self-Evaluation.* Based upon student indicators of learning, what adjustments, if any, do you need to make for the next lesson? If you were to teach that same lesson again, what were the strengths, and what changes would you make to refine the lesson?

teachers, inexperienced or otherwise. Nevertheless, lesson-plan purists persist in believing that traditional plans are a powerful, positive influence capable of molding teacher behavior in appropriate ways and are, therefore, a key component of teacher preparation.

Moderates on the issue of lesson planning may require plans of teachers-in-training, but they do not think a written plan, in and of itself, is particularly powerful. They would argue that "a lesson plan is not a real lesson. It is, however, one way of getting close to the normative idea of what was expected to take place in the actual teaching process" (Linné, 2001a, p. 135). A moderate position on planning considers teaching to be too complex to be brought under control by a bit of thinking on paper. Moderates would connect teachers' plans with students' understanding, as reflected in the following definition:

> Lesson planning can be defined as preactive decision making that takes place before instruction. Cognizant decision making, such as lesson planning, involves teachers' conscious efforts in developing a coherent system of activities that promote the development of students' cognitive structures. Planning a meaningful experience for students is a basic requirement for successful teaching. (Panasuk, Stone, & Todd, 2002, p. 808)

In this view, lesson planning is cyclic, recursive, and somewhat improvisational (Borko & Livingston, 1989; Leinhardt & Greeno, 1986; Pinnegar, 1988; Yinger, 1987). Additionally, lesson planning is influenced by the teacher's prior classroom experiences (not merely as a teacher but also as a student) and is affected by the subject matter, grade level, and available resources within a particular context—school, community, and culture (Clark & Yinger, 1979a, 1979b, 1987; Yinger, 1980). Above all, in the absence of reflective practice (Dewey, 1933; Eby, Herrell, & Jordan, 2005), the plan is just an outline, a proposal, a form of mental rehearsal. Moderates on lesson planning favor some latitude in the format of plans and argue for increased functionality (Kagan & Tippins, 1992). In addition, they point out that teaching is much more than delivering a body of content to learners.

> One might assume that once teachers have a personal understanding of their content, they are ready to teach it to children. This is rarely the case. Besides finding their own meaning, teachers must find ways to make the content important and meaningful to students. They cannot simply tell students what they have figured out for themselves. Even when teachers work with prepared materials, they still have to clarify what they want students to learn, anticipate how students are likely to respond, and adapt teaching suggestions to fit their own situation. (Dorph, 1997, p. 470)

This more collaborative and flexible approach to planning is reflected in a modified version of Japanese lesson study. Figure 1.2 is an example of a lesson plan that was influenced by this approach. (To examine, in depth, a project with teachers that implemented lesson study, see Celeste Campbell's [2002] Lesson Study Research Project posted at http://www. tc.columbia.edu/lessonstudy/worksharing.html

---

Figure 1.2 Sample Lesson Plan Using Collaborative Approaches

Grade: 9

Class: Algebra

Instructor: Mr. Jim Preston

I.   Background information

    A.   Goal of the lesson study group:

        The goal of the lesson study group is to create a lesson that helps the student relate abstract algebraic calculations to concrete situations. In the past, students tended to try to memorize certain algorithms for manipulating variables and as a result often had only a superficial understanding of the rules of algebra and seldom recalled these algorithms for any extended period of time.

    B.   Narrative overview of background information:

        The students in this classroom have been involved with five chapters of Algebra II study. There are various levels of student achievement and motivation in the classroom. As a class we have made great strides in creating an environment of student exploration, and there is a culture of support from one student to another with regard to mathematical achievement. Students often try the guess, check, and revise method as a first course of action when attempting to solve a problem but have been developing many other tools for problem solving throughout the school year.

II. Unit information

    A.   Name of the unit:

        Polynomials and polynomial functions

    B.   Goal(s) of the unit:

        • Use properties of exponents to evaluate and simplify expressions

        • Use exponents and scientific notation in real-life situations

        • Evaluate polynomial functions

        • Graph polynomial functions

        • Add, subtract, and multiply polynomials

        • Use polynomial operations in real-life situations

- Factor polynomial expressions
- Use factoring to solve polynomial equations
- Divide polynomials and relate the results to the remainder theorem
- Use polynomial division in real-life situations
- Find the rational zeros of a polynomial function
- Use polynomial equations in real-life situations
- Use technology to approximate the zeros of a polynomial function
- Analyze the graph of polynomial functions
- Use the graph of a polynomial function to answer questions about real-life situations
- Use technology to find polynomial models for real-life data

C. How this unit is related to the curriculum:

Much of the mathematics taught in the high school setting is about relationships. Polynomials are commonly used forms to describe relationships in the real world. Manipulations of polynomial expressions are necessary in understanding various relationships as well as achieving success in future mathematics courses.

D. Instructional sequence for the unit:

This lesson occurs in section 3 of a 9-section unit. The ultimate goal of the unit is for students to study the relationship described by polynomial functions. In order to do this, students need to be able to manipulate algebraic expressions. Students also will need to be able to factor polynomials, and being able to multiply polynomial expressions with facility will allow students to better understand the factoring process.

III. Lesson information

A. Name of the study lesson:

Expanding binomial expressions

B. Goal(s) of the study lesson:

Students will use the pattern in the expansion of binomial expressions to expand binomials when raised to various exponents.

Students will relate polynomial expressions to area and volume.

C. How this study lesson is related to the lesson study goal:

This lesson will use rectangular solids to help students see the expansion of $(a + b)^3$ in a manner that goes beyond the simple manipulations of symbols. It is hoped that this process will enable the students to remember the relationship better and see algebraic identities in a different light than they are accustomed to.

D. Process of the study lesson:

Steps of the lesson: learning activities and key questions (and time allocation)	Student activities/ expected student reactions or responses	Teacher's response to student reactions/Things to remember	Goals and method(s) of evaluation
Distribute the manipulatives (1 min.)	Students will need to pick up eight rectangular solids	The teacher may want to give students a little time to get the urge to build with the blocks out of their systems	
The teacher will ask the students to determine the volume of each of the rectangular solids in terms of the variables a and b (7 min.)	"Don't we need a ruler to measure the sides?"	Students may not completely understand how to determine the volume in terms of variables and the teacher will need to clarify	
The teacher should move from student to student or group to group to make sure they understand the task	In pairs or groups, students should determine the volume of each of the four distinct pieces in terms of a and b		The teacher should see students talking about how to find the volume of each piece. They should be drawing pictures in their notes and labeling their volume in terms of a and b
After it appears that all students have an answer for the volume of each of the four distinct pieces, the teacher and students will discuss the results. Sketches of each of the pieces will be drawn on the chalkboard and their volumes will be determined (8 min.)	Students should respond to the teacher's questions about what they found as the volumes of each of the pieces	See Appendix for example of boardwork	
Students will then be asked to create a cube using the eight pieces (5 min.)			

After each student or group has successfully created the cube, they will be asked to determine the volume of the large cube in terms of a and b (5 min.).		"Now create one large cube using all of the eight pieces you have. You must use all pieces and you cannot use the pieces from another person's set of blocks."	
Students will be asked to think about the relationship between the volume of the eight pieces and the one large cube (4 min.)	"Do we have to use all of the pieces?"		The students should be trying various configurations to get the parts to make one large cube
At this point the teacher will ask students to apply the relationship established by the examination of volumes to various binomials. The teacher will check with each student or group as he walks around the room. Solutions will be discussed (15 min.)	"Are you sure this is possible?"	Clarify the following: $(a + b)^3 =$ $a^3 + 3a^2b + 3ab^2 + b^3$	
	The students hopefully will conclude that the sum of the volumes of the individual pieces is equal to the volume of the large cube	Ask students to specifically say how the volumes are equal	
	"They're equal"	Help students clarify their thoughts	Students should be writing the relationship down in their notebooks
	Students will use this relationship to expand $(x + 2)^3$ $(y - 3)^3$ $(a + 1)^3$ $(2x - 5)^3$	Allow several students to state their findings before solidifying the relationship	The teacher will walk around and help students who are struggling
An extension to this lesson that should be continued in the next lesson will involve the application of Pascal's Triangle to the expansion of a binomial to various exponents of higher value		The teacher should ask students how the activity with the blocks might help them with expanding the cube of a binomial	Students should indicate that the activity will be memorable

E. Evaluation:

$$(x + 2)^3$$
$$(y - 3)^3$$
$$(a + 1)^3$$
$$(2x - 5)^3$$

Students will be asked to create a geometric representation for $(a + b)^2$ as homework. The in-class activities also will be used to evaluate student understanding, as will an end-of-the-unit test and periodic subsequent quizzes.

$(a + b)^2$

a^2 $2ab$ b^2

F.   Appendix:

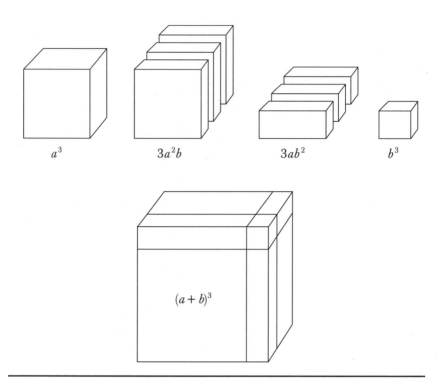

a^3 $3a^2b$ $3ab^2$ b^3

$(a+b)^3$

A third and final group considers traditional lesson plans to be an impediment to progress that drags down teachers' thinking and reduces it to behaviorist approaches (cf., Zeegers, 2000). The worldview of this group is aligned with critical pedagogy. For them, it makes little sense to plan a careful, teacher-directed sequence of events in the midst of a diverse group of learners and an unpredictable classroom context; for them, teaching is more than covering content and more even than reflecting on practice. From a critical pedagogy perspective, planning should be a way of challenging the status quo and empowering learners.

Consistent with this perspective, Mosenthal (1986) uses street theater as a metaphor for teaching. A busy downtown street offers many competing demands on attention; the goal of street theater is first, to attract interest that causes passersby to pause; next, to engage the minds and hearts of the audience in ways that encourage them to linger and participate; and ultimately, to send them on their way, changed for the better. Both for street theater and for teaching, transformation is part of the plan.

To further support their contention that teacher planning, as most of us know it, must be reconceptualized, these critics point to the behavior of teachers who, by anyone's definition, are at the top of their fields, such as the remarkable classroom teachers studied indepth by Richhart (2003) or the Nobel Prize laureate and highly celebrated college instructor Richard Feynman (1997).

From a critical pedagogy perspective, the overarching goal of lessons is to engage learners in social action. Linear lesson plans are a straightjacket that restrains voice and restricts choice for learners and teachers (Christensen, 2002; Vasquez, 2003). If teachers in the United States were to emulate the Japanese lesson meeting approach in its entirety, planning would venture into the realm of critical pedagogy by transforming the culture of the school. The Teachers College website (http://www.tc.columbia.edu/lessonstudy) offers an example of a project that is faithful to the precepts of the Japanese lesson meeting and has been sustained over an extended period of time.

What appears to be the common ground among those who would throw out, those who would modify, and those who cling to traditional lesson plans is good intentions. All are seeking to provide a much-needed scaffold for student learning and teacher effectiveness. Yet, in order for that scaffold to be helpful, it needs to rest on solid ground. For a teacher—particularly an inexperienced teacher—filling in the blanks on a lesson plan provides the merest form of support because, as we will argue throughout this book, it rests on shaky ground. A firmer foundation is the collective, collegial wisdom of a group of teachers. That foundation might be strengthened further by the contributions of teacher educators with a commitment to basic education who participate, not just to complete a research project, but to develop a long-term, sustainable, and productive collaboration, such as those seen in exemplary Professional Development Schools (Teitel, 2003).

The tie that binds enthusiasts of the traditional lesson plan, moderates on lesson planning, and those who approach planning from a critical pedagogy perspective is their desire to support teachers, both novice and experienced, in achieving their full potential as educators, thereby promoting the learning of all students. In fact, this commitment to promote learning for oneself, one's colleagues, and all children is what the Greeks referred to as the *telos*, the prime directive, of teacher educators. Collaborative planning is a way of actualizing those good intentions because it is the interface of theory/research and practice, a space where professors reconnect with the practical, day-to-day concerns of classroom teachers, while teachers have a chance to catch their breath, step back, and become more analytical. If educators neglect to do this, the chasm between theory/research and practice widens, while basic and higher education drift apart. When lessons fail, education fails. Failed lessons do not constitute a single, dramatic loss, but their cumulative effect is to weaken the teaching/learning process and the effectiveness of the educational system. Students fail subjects, repeat grade levels, and drop out of school, while teachers abandon the career in record numbers. This waste of human capital alone is sufficient justification to challenge the myth of lesson planning.

THE CASE AGAINST TRADITIONAL LESSON PLANNING

We contend that lesson planning as it is commonly practiced and understood in teacher preparation institutions, state departments of education, and national curricula has outlived its usefulness. Evidently, the limitations of the traditional lesson plan are apparent even to preservice teachers. A group of 18 education majors who had produced written plans (but not yet taught them) discussed problems with lesson planning. Some of their comments were:

- "I don't know how to make sure it is age-appropriate so that the students will understand the lesson. It is difficult to estimate the length of the lesson. There are also problems with ways to assess what you've taught."
- "There's no basis for putting together a lesson for first time."
- "Unpredictability is a problem I have encountered. Sometimes you may have thought of a wonderful plan and the students just don't get the concept."
- "No teacher has the time to write immaculate lesson plans. No teacher has every single day planned out with a 4-page plan for every activity—although time to do so would be ideal."
- "I believe that time is of the essence in planning, and I believe that teachers probably will be spending personal time planning if they wish to succeed."
- "Lesson planning is very time-consuming and what you write down to teach doesn't always end up the way you would like. My concern is putting a lot of effort into something and being unsuccessful."

As these comments suggest, these students are well aware of the limitations of traditional lesson plans, even before they begin to teach from them. The assertions that follow, bolstered by research in the field, build a case against typical lesson plans.

Typical Plans Ignore Important Distinctions in Teachers' Ways of Knowing

In 1977, Harry Broudy suggested three ways of knowing: "knowing that," "knowing how," and "knowing with." The lowest level, "knowing that," refers to a replication of what was learned in much the same fashion as it was learned (e.g., following the teacher's manual). "Knowing how" moves into the application level as a solution is deduced from facts, rules, and principles that have been learned. The teacher who is capable of reviewing many different resources and producing a plan without a template to follow, knows how. The third and most sophisticated category, "knowing with," is closer to contemporary expectations for teachers because it takes the context for learning and the individual learners into account. It involves expectations, judgment, shaping the response, enriching or elaborating on what is there, and reorganizing the situation—all things that effective teachers do.

Typical Plans Promote an Information-Giving Type of Pedagogy

In their study of the lesson logs and plans of 12 student teachers, Kagan and Tippins (1992) concluded that the traditional lesson plan was "counterproductive." Plans drove secondary student teachers, who tended to be more content-oriented than elementary student teachers, to an overreliance on textbooks, lectures, and tests. Additionally, after secondary student teachers had developed linear plans, they tended to avoid improvisation and struggled to follow the plans even when lessons were not progressing as the teachers had anticipated.

Plans created a different sort of conundrum for elementary student teachers who, as a group, tended to be more student-needs-oriented. For elementary student teachers, linear plans stood in the way of integrating the curriculum and engaging students. Even more problematic, lockstep lesson plans sometimes caused student teachers to feel that they had failed if they did not follow the plans.

The shortcomings of linear plans are underscored when lessons center on objectives from the affective domain. In a study of preservice teachers' ability to write plans that met multicultural standards, plans that incorporated worthy goals such as multicultural knowledge, dispositions, and performance were the rare exception; most approached multicultural education as delivering information (M. Miller, 2001). Linear plans tend to promote the notion of "teaching as telling."

Typical Plans Fail to Represent Teachers' Mental Planning Processes

An analysis of the historical origins and social construction of a phenomenon is necessary in order to understand it (Popkewitz, 1997), and lesson plans are no exception. Traditional approaches to planning echo the behaviorist origins of the lesson plan. Historical studies of teacher planning have found that plans produced decades ago by experienced teachers are barely distinguishable from those produced by practicing teachers today (Linné, 2001a, 2001b). Teacher preparation institutions devote instructional time to teaching novices how to write traditional lesson plans, and commit institutional resources to supervisory personnel who are obligated to make certain that the plans are followed (Clark & Peterson, 1986). All of this is done even though teachers abandon, at the earliest opportunity, the lesson planning models so painstakingly taught in methods courses (Clark & Peterson, 1986; Clark & Yinger, 1979a, 1979b). In fact, when the planning processes of exemplary teachers are the focus, highly idiosyncratic and complex mind maps, rather than predictable formulas, characterize their thinking (Richhart, 2003). In general, the literature suggests that there is a rift between written plans and teachers' internal planning processes.

> Teachers envision themselves enacting the plan, what they will say, questions they will ask, when to pass out what materials, where they will stand, how to arrange the students, and they anticipate potential difficulties and how to deal with them, among other matters they consider. So, when teachers plan, their plans and planning do not follow linear models included in some teacher education preservice courses where teachers are to write objectives, materials needed, then the instructional procedure, plans for student practice and evaluation. (McCutcheon & Milner, 2002, pp. 81–82)

Linear plans are not sufficiently capacious to accommodate the level of reasoning required of contemporary teachers.

Typical Plans Are Taught "Objectives First" but Produced "Activities First"

As noted above, most advocates of traditional lesson plans insist that behavioral objectives are the starting point. In a review of the literature on teacher planning by Newfield (1982), a common finding was that teachers seldom began with the objectives; rather, they focused on activities, content, or both. This theme in the research certainly is consistent with the daily experience of teacher educators who work with college students.

More often than not, a novice teacher's starting point for a lesson is whatever materials are readily available. It is not uncommon for novice teachers to appear at faculty members' office doors, eager to borrow a children's book and build a lesson around it, or for preservice teachers to begin the planning process by trolling the Internet in search of ideas for activities.

Student teachers and novices seem to have trouble linking activities with objectives. One student was attempting to teach the skills of interviewing by making himself the subject of the interview. He brought his soccer ball to school and demonstrated some impressive moves, but the lesson never quite got around to teaching the children how to plan an interview and ask good questions. When asked to self-evaluate, the student said, "The kids really seemed interested and paid attention." This lesson was long on activity and very short on objectives or concept development. The traditional lesson plan does little to alter a preoccupation with "What do I do Monday?" or superficial content coverage.

Typical Plans Mask Subject Matter Incompetence

Another limitation of the traditional lesson plan is that preparing it does not guarantee sufficient teacher background in the content. Bischoff, Hatch, and Watford's (1999) study of planning concluded that preservice teachers reported being well aware of their content weaknesses in science and math and willing to admit to these deficiencies. Nevertheless, these preservice teachers could offer no clear evidence that they made an effort to learn the content and, instead of working to fill in the gaps in their knowledge, they lowered their expectations for student achievement. They seem to have been able to generate a passable, traditional lesson plan without mastering the content, a finding that was consistent with another study of students' attempts to teach the scientific concept of combustion (De Jong, Ahtee, Goodwin, Hatzinkita, & Koulaidis, 1999). Linear plans can camouflage teachers' subject-matter limitations.

Typical Plans Only Imply Pedagogy

Even high levels of subject-matter expertise do not guarantee that the pedagogical strategies outlined in the lesson plan are a suitable "match" for the particular learner or the specific subject matter. Teaching well demands pedagogical content knowledge, defined as

> understanding the central topics in each subject as it is generally taught to children of a particular grade level and being able to ask the following

kinds of questions about each topic: what are core concepts, skills, and attitudes which this topic has the potential of conveying to students? . . . What students' preconceptions are likely to get in the way of learning? (Shulman & Sykes, 1986, p. 9)

Success in teaching demands more than content mastery, more even than pedagogical content knowledge, yet behavioristic plans suggest otherwise. The brevity of most plans makes the underlying pedagogy difficult to ascertain.

Typical Plans Are Accomplished Single-Handedly

Given the charge of teaching to higher standards, consultation among educators is a necessary first step in producing quality plans that result in the higher student achievement needed to attain adequate yearly progress (Litde & Crawford, 2002). The difficulty with planning in isolation is that "teachers may gain understandings of a specific strategy or process and fail to see the connections between and among them that result in more effective practice. Through continuous feedback and engagement these connections are established and maintained" (Jinkins, 2001, p. 283). A more enlightened view would be to treat the lesson plan as a carefully crafted and classroom-tested document that has been enriched by a thoughtful analysis of learners' responses and peers' insights (Kärräinen, 2000). Participation in collegial discussions of plans engages teachers in shaping learning opportunities for students, deepening understanding in learners, and making the teaching/learning process immediate and relevant for their students as well as for themselves (Dorph, 1997). Even excellent plans that are generated in solitude by individual educators fail to realize their full potential for the grade level, district, or profession by restricting expertise to the confines of a single classroom.

Typical Plans Assume Common Expectations for Students

Implicit in the traditional plan is the expectation that students' responses will be similar, or at least predictable. When behavioral objectives were in their heyday during the 1960s and 1970s, it was not unusual for plans to specify the level of performance expected and indicate, for example, that children could identify the parts of a plant "with 80% accuracy." Every teacher has seen a teachers' manual that parenthetically suggests how the students ought to respond to a question, another indicator of common expectations. In fact, linear plans were so ill suited to the adaptations necessary when working with students who have special needs that completely different structures, such as the individualized educational plan, were used. An interesting strand in the professional development literature of the United Kingdom is a concept called variation. The premise is that in order to change teachers' understanding of teaching, it is essential to focus on the variation in students' experience of the object of learning (Pong, 2001; Wood, 2000). Variation begins with the assumption that students' responses will be characterized by difference rather than sameness. Its goal is for teachers to engage with change in their teaching to the benefit of the students by addressing some of their questions. Assumptions of variation are that:

- students' unique ways of experiencing the object of learning help to develop ideas about their levels of understanding;
- teaching strategies must take account of this variation and cannot be prescribed independently of it;
- transfer can be achieved by learning to experience variation in what is critical to understanding;
- students become comfortable with exploring their understandings in contexts where variation is valued. (Wood, 2003, p. 212)

Current calls for "teacher-proof," scripted lessons—those most insulting of instructional materials—are the antithesis of planned variation.

Typical Plans Overemphasize the Novice/Expert Dichotomy

The challenge that faces contemporary teachers at all levels of experience is to generate lessons that are, in the words of the National Council for the Social Studies (1994), "meaningful, integrative, value-based, challenging, and active" (p. 162). As O'Mahony (2003) observes:

> Perhaps expecting teacher candidates to consider children's thinking when they plan is asking too much. After all, they are novices who are focused on their "performance" as teachers rather than experienced professionals who measure their success by evidence of student learning as well as engagement in lessons. (p. 256)

The challenge facing veteran teachers may be no less formidable, however. Experienced educators today are expected to "unlearn" much of what is routine and comfortable about planning. When the goal is to generate lessons that not only captivate students' interest but also result in forms of concept development that translate into higher levels of achievement, the vastly experienced, "follow the book"-type of teacher may be no better off than a novice. Moreover, for teachers at every level of experience, it is important to maintain that important distinction between competence and performance. A teacher may be capable of high levels of competence yet decide, for a variety of reasons, not to perform at those high levels. Novice or expert aside, influences such as personal crises, fear of failure, oppressive school cultures, and a host of other variables can impede peak performance.

MOVING BEYOND THE LINEAR LESSON PLAN

Returning to the "horror story" that began this chapter, imagine if the student teacher instead had relied on a plan carefully crafted using the collective professional wisdom of a group of teachers familiar with her grade level. Imagine that, instead of staring at a blank computer screen back in her dormitory room, this student teacher had been a full-fledged participant in a planning meeting that provided her with opportunities for reflective practice. Collaborative lesson planning is an appropriate "next step" in the progression of ideas about the critical role that planning plays in effective teaching.

Ultimately, effective teaching demands that teachers at all levels learn to meet the challenge of "orchestrating the unpredictable" (Hiebert & Stigler, 2000, p. 3). Collaborative, collegial planning offers the greatest promise for supporting teachers in rising to that challenge. One approach would be to emulate lesson study as it is practiced in Japan. Stated plainly, education in the United States has a very disappointing track record in taking powerful educational ideas from other countries and implementing them successfully. There is a tendency to focus on the most superficial aspects of the innovation and to confuse educational means with ends (Egan, 1989). Take, for example, the British Infant Schools that led the Open Education Movement of the 1970s. Some teacher educators immediately sought to be identified as the experts who were in a position to decide whether the concept was being implemented appropriately. They approached their task with an almost religious zeal and were harshly critical of any attempt that did not imitate the schools in Great Britain in every conceivable way. Meanwhile, back in the elementary schools, many misguided educators took the "open school" label quite literally and began constructing new buildings without walls, completely missing the point that openness referred to the curriculum and student choice of activity rather than architectural features of a building. A similar scenario threatens to play out once again, except that this time it is with the Japanese lesson meeting. Figure 1.3 is an overview of the essential elements of the Japanese lesson meeting that we find pertinent to our discussion of collaborative lesson planning.

Figure 1.3 A Modified Approach to Lesson Study

Select a Worthwhile Goal. Teachers from one or more schools agree upon a goal that they all want to achieve with their students. Often, such goals are framed as a question. Goals are rooted in real data: observations, analyses of students' responses to assignments, interviews with or surveys of students, or special assessments to identify areas that need growth. When deciding what goals and lessons are worthy of such development, teachers often identify a concept that is taught across the grade levels, a difficult concept, or something that students tend to find boring (but that they need to master).

Study Students' Work and Develop a Plan. Teachers consider the difficulties encountered by their students, begin brainstorming practical solutions, and generate a plan. Teachers participate in an inquiry to determine approaches that would narrow the gap between students' performance and teacher's aspirations for them. At this point, it is often helpful for teachers to survey other teachers concerning what they have done in similar circumstances.

Teach and Observe the Collaborative Lesson. One teacher uses the plan to teach while others observe. The focus of these observations is absolutely crucial: *The goal is not to evaluate the teacher; it is to analyze the lesson's effectiveness in promoting student learning.* This perspective runs counter to virtually every experience U.S. teachers have had with observation, commencing with the earliest student teaching experiences and continuing through their evaluations by supervisors as seasoned veterans, so everyone must understand at the outset that collaborative lesson review stands observation on its head by making students the focal point. After the study lesson has been tried the first time, another planning session is scheduled.

Discuss and Reflect. Members of the group meet to discuss their observations and reflect on what they have learned about the goal they set out to explore. Some tips for dealing with debates: Teachers who are doing the teaching have the deciding vote on which strategy they will try first. A potential pitfall of discussions is engaging in lengthy, unproductive pedagogical debates. Here it is best to concentrate on evaluating evidence from a particular lesson and render decisions that are driven by student performance data that emanated from the lesson. Some questions that keep the group on task include: What is our goal here? What are we trying to learn about? What do we want our students to do?

Develop the Lesson Further. The original lesson is subjected to in-depth analysis as it is taught, revised, and retaught. Discussion often leads to a revision of the plan and reteaching of the lesson by another group member while others observe. Teachers work as a group (e.g., 4–6 teachers, small groups reporting back to large groups) to produce a detailed lesson plan. The goal is to engage in honest, productive discussions; often, it is helpful to have a protocol to follow. All of the teachers who planned the lesson report back on the outcomes with their students, not just the one who taught it for others to observe. The group decides whether it would be helpful to invite an outside advisor, such as a university faculty member, to visit the group periodically and provide support.

Disseminate the Polished Plan. Teachers produce a record of their lesson study work by composing a reflective report; the teachers who actually taught the lesson take the lead in writing the plan. The group also may hold an open house periodically where they share their work with other school staff and invited guests. In Japan, these reports sometimes are published as brochures, monographs, or research articles, and bookstores in Japan overflow with them. These published works are artifacts that document deep and grounded reflection about the complex activities of teaching (adapted from Fernandez & Chokshi, 2002).

According to innovation theory (Hord, Rutherford, Huling-Austin, & Hall, 1998), in order for an innovation to be adopted and sustained, both the organization and the innovation itself must be modified somewhat. From this theoretical perspective, then, it might be possible to incorporate some of the practices represented by the Japanese lesson meeting without following the procedure slavishly. Rather than forcing Japanese lesson study to fit a completely different culture and school system, we have decided to concentrate on the best that lesson study has to offer, namely, collaborative planning, an emphasis on concept development for learners, and an inquiry stance among the teachers.

ENGAGING TEACHERS IN LESSON DESIGN AND REVIEW

Our first foray into collaborative planning was inspired by the teacher-as-researcher work of Marilyn Cochran-Smith and Susan Lytle (1993). We began with a group of practicing teachers who were enrolled in a program that enabled them to earn a second teaching certificate as well as a master's degree in education. These part-time students progressed through the same courses at the same time as a cohort, and the group was in its third and final year of study, so they knew and trusted one another.

The assignment was for each student to identify two lessons that they considered to have been a failure and to seek constructive criticism from peers. They were then asked to revise the lesson based on the recommendations from their classmates, reteach the lesson, and provide "before and after" examples of students' responses to the lesson. At first, this was a very disconcerting proposition. Teachers in the United States are pressured to, as one student put it, "make it up as we go along." This assignment challenged teachers to expose their ignorance and to admit that, even as experienced and respected educators, they did not always feel competent or confident.

Guiding Lesson Choice

The first challenge in the peer review of lessons was to convince the teachers that they had to choose a lesson that failed. This contradicted just about everything that they previously had done in classes and in schools. As teachers, we are accustomed to putting together portfolios of our best work, rather than talking about our mistakes or misgivings openly. Figure 1.4 contains the guidelines that were distributed to students well in advance of the first class meeting, to give everyone a chance to think about this unusual assignment and collect examples of children's work (with the children's names blotted out for confidentiality's sake). Teachers felt cautious at first and chose a lesson they already had some ideas about how to fix. With additional reviews of lessons by peers, however, they started to feel freer to select lessons that had confounded them.

Configuring Groups

Prior to the class, students were clustered together in groups of approximately six members. At first, the teachers suggested groupings based on grade-level assignments. Yet when the goal was to break out of customary ways of thinking, we found that it was best to structure the groups to be as diverse as possible. Kindergarten teachers, for example, have a "shared" repertoire of ideas about teaching kindergarten and they benefited from a special educator's or an art teacher's perspectives on their "problem lesson."

Sharing the Lessons

Before the groups assembled for the first time, the instructor emphasized that their goal was professional development. Therefore, three types of responses were unacceptable:

1. Offering no feedback (e.g., saying the lesson is fine as is)
2. Criticizing without constructive suggestions
3. Getting defensive about others' recommendations

It was also important to caution the teachers about dwelling on issues that were outside their control. Freedman (2001) found that when three teacher research groups met (one focusing on literacy in four urban settings, one from three schools in the San Francisco Bay area, and the other for first-year teachers), teachers tended to talk freely about extrinsic barriers to effective teaching (e.g., violence in society, lack of parental involvement,

---

Figure 1.4 Procedure for Peer Review of Lesson Plans

The purpose of this assignment is to use your colleagues as resource people who can contribute to your professional development as you revise a lesson that failed. The goal is to gain multiple perspectives on teaching strategies and make modifications that make the lesson more effective with diverse groups of students. This idea is adapted from the teacher-as-researcher work of Marilyn Cochran-Smith and Susan Lytle.

First, identify a lesson you have taught that was *less than satisfactory*. Bring in six copies of your original plan and, if available, examples of student responses that reflect high, moderate, and low attainment of the objective. Remove all identifying information from the students' papers. Meet with classmates to brainstorm alternatives and solutions. Revise the lesson accordingly. Create a table that highlights the proposed changes in the lesson. Then reteach the lesson and bring in student work samples that reflect a range of responses from the learners. Write 1–2 paragraphs summarizing what you learned from the peer review experience. Turn in (1) the original plan, (2) the table, (3) the 1–2 paragraph analysis, and (4) the student work samples. Do this for four lessons during the semester.

The Roles

- *Teacher*: Each teacher is required to bring six copies of a lesson that she or he has taught and a representative sampling of students' responses to the lesson. (Conceal the students' names.) The teacher makes a 3- to 4-minute presentation on the lesson to the study group.

- *Peer Reviewers*: Peers are expected to (1) listen, (2) raise questions, (3) analyze student work samples provided by the teacher that illustrate the gamut of students' performance, and (4) offer concrete suggestions, based on their wisdom of practice. The goal is to make the concepts more understandable and meaningful for the students.

- *Procedures*: The entire process should take about 30 minutes and follow this sequence: introduction of group members, presentation by teacher, questions and comments from peers, analysis of students' work, peer feedback (the teacher's role during this phase is to listen and take notes, not defend), reflections on peer recommendations from the teacher, and discussion/conclusion.

The Written Reports of the Peer Reviews of Lessons

At the end of the process, every teacher will produce a report that highlights key recommendations from the study group, the changes that were made, and the outcomes for students. Here is an example:

Situation: A first-grade teacher is having difficulty getting across the concept of a missing addend in problems such as $3 + ? = 5$.

Recommendations from Peers	Modifications by Teacher	Outcomes for Students
"Have you ever tried using a numberline? I use flashcards and show them a problem, then they tell me how many jumps they had to make to get to the answer."	I tried each of the more concrete methods recommended. We used the numberline made out of tape on the floor first. I have a very lively group and thought this might get them interested and motivated. I purposely made the spaces between the numbers rather large so that everyone could see and to maximize the opportunity to jump.	On the first workbook page of missing addends, only 8 of my 26 students had the concept. By the second day, after the numberline on the floor, 16 had nearly all of the problems correct.
"Yes, I even used tape on the floor to make a numberline so that all children could see and participate in figuring out the answer. Then I switched to small laminated number lines on their desks."	The next day, each child was given one small plastic counter to use to hop to the answers on the numberline on their desks. I kept asking, "How many hops?" I noticed that some children weren't counting the hops correctly and had to emphasize that a hop consisted of the *move* from one number to the next. I think some are so accustomed to being told not to forget to count themselves when counting that they were counting the number they started at, so I corrected this with a small group back at the numberline on the floor.	After the second day of practice, 20 students had all or nearly all problems correct. With supervised practice at the numberline with the remaining 6, four of them were able to figure out the answers. Two were still experiencing difficulty.
"Try making it more concrete. I use those little plastic teddybear counters and have them count out loud with me on several practice items. I make practice sheets with boxes in them big enough to put the counters. They place them there, then write the answer and hold it up for me to see."	As a large group practice, I used the worksheet with the counters so that children had yet another concrete way to figure out the missing addend.	This playful way of getting to the answer appealed to the children. Although I doubt that all of the students have the concept firmly implanted, all were able to experience some level of success with missing addend problems.

administrative incompetence). However, teachers "varied in their comfort levels in talking about intrinsic problems—such as their ability to control the class, difficulties teaching certain types of students, and their failures in getting students interested in grappling with difficult curricular material" (p. 193). As a "friendly critic" (L. Miller, 2001), the teacher educator's goal during the peer review of lessons is to gently get teachers focused on the issues over which they have some control and urge teachers to venture into territory with "wiggle room"—that curricular space where teachers can exercise greater autonomy (Bullough & Gitlin, 2001).

As each group member shared a lesson and samples of the students' responses with their peers, he or she was expected to listen carefully to their advice and take notes. For instance, Heather reported that her first graders were having difficulty with the concept of more and less. As Lisa studied a set of the children's papers, she noticed that "every child got the last one correct." The group decided that the reason children got it correct was that it was such a dramatic example, with one group containing eight hats and the other only two. So the suggestion was to reintroduce the concept to the children who were having difficulty, only this time to use several dramatic examples to establish the concept, and build on that success.

Despite advice about the peer review process, there were still occasional blushes of embarrassment or startled facial expressions during these discussions. Many teachers are so concerned about being "nice," taken to mean never uttering a discouraging word about anything, that they just aren't accustomed to talking to one another about disappointing outcomes for lessons. Sometimes, a fairly obvious solution eluded them and their reaction to a colleague's recommendation was, "Why didn't *I* think of that?" To break down these barriers, the instructor shared examples of teaching mistakes (including her own) that earned knowing looks and smiles of amusement. Some published sources for going public with teaching mistakes are *Oops! What We Do When Our Teaching Fails* (Power & Hubbard, 1996) and *This Teaching Life: How I Taught Myself to Teach* (Wassermann, 2004), in which well-known educators/authors admit to their mistakes as teachers. As teachers collaborate, they can see how their colleagues

> construct problems, wrestle with uncertainty, change their minds about long-established practices or assumptions, gather evidence and examples for analysis and interpretation, connect pieces of information to one another, and develop interpretive frameworks for the daily work of teaching. (Cochran-Smith, 2004, p. 13)

It is particularly important for the teacher educator to circulate among these groups, listen in, and provide additional opinions—not offered as the "official answer," but from the stance of another experienced teacher's input. There are no absolute answers here. Rather, there should be a sense of possibility, a climate for promoting positive change, and role models of resilience. The instructor also might take this opportunity to observe collaborative planning processes in action. Teacher educators can use a simple grid that includes the five stages in team planning identified by Friedland and Walz (2003) to organize notes and comments, realizing that a team could be working at different stages in a single meeting. The stages are:

1. Establishing a team
2. Identifying the problem
3. Generating interventions
4. Planning intervention implementation
5. Evaluating the proposed intervention

Presenting Results from Retaught Lessons

The next step occurred when the experienced teachers/graduate students returned with the results of their retaught lessons. They shared a list of the key suggestions from the study group and explained how they incorporated them into the revision. Additionally, they had collected a new set of children's work. After the groups met to hear about the revised lessons, everyone searched for recurring themes in the before and after assignments, and the total group generated the list of recommendations in Figure 1.5.

Gradually, teachers warmed to the peer review of lesson plans. In fact, it became the top-ranked activity in their 3-year program because, unlike some assignments in graduate school, it was directly applicable to their daily lives in classrooms.

*   *   *

Lesson planning is an activity in which all teachers engage. Although a lesson plan may not be a particularly accurate guide to what actually happens in the classroom, it does at least demonstrate "intention to act" (Ajzen & Fishbein, 1980). Through planning, experienced teachers translate academic standards, institutional expectations, and personal/professional philosophy into action (Calderhead, 1984). Planning is also a useful indicator by which to judge the practice and development of novices, because it gives access to a "focus of personal theory and professional thinking . . . at the interface of belief and practice" (Tann, 1993, p. 56, quoted in Davies & Rogers, 2000). The benefits of planning collaboratively and teaching for

---

Figure 1.5 What Teachers Can Do When Students Don't Understand

Check Definitions. Define terminology clearly at the outset using an *authoritative* source. For instance, if you want to teach the concept of a "home," how do you define the term *home*? It is not the same as a house, and it is not synonymous with habitat.

Check Understanding with Counterinstances. It is not enough to say what a concept is; you also have to be able to say what it is not. Unless children can differentiate between pairs of words that rhyme and those that do not, they do not understand the concept. They need practice with counterinstances to show what they know.

Clarify Concepts. Figure out the essential understandings that underlie a concept, such as terms, facts, and principles (Kostelnik, 1991). Terms are the key definitions, facts are generally undisputed information about a concept, and principles are the inferences that the learners need to make in order to grasp the concept.

Anticipate Difficulties. Providing an effective explanation does not consist simply of breaking down a process into component parts; teachers also need to anticipate when difficulties may arise. One first-grade teacher whose students were constructing riddle books with a lift-the-flap feature could foresee that some children would start cutting out the flap and forget to leave one side attached. She decided to avoid this by showing the students several books and greeting cards with flaps that lifted. She pointed out where the hinge had to be so that children could think about how they wanted the flap to operate.

Discuss the Rationale. Before beginning a project, children need to understand the purpose. A teacher who was working with children to design the front and back covers for the books they had written brought in examples of many distinctive front and back covers. Questions she raised were: How are these book covers alike? How are they different? Why do books have covers? What information is usually contained on the front cover? On the back? What new ideas do you have for your book cover?

Make It Relevant. An undeniable part of teaching is helping children to see the connections between what they are learning and their daily lives. A second-grade teacher who was teaching a lesson on water had a hard time explaining condensation. The big breakthrough came when she began the lesson by saying, "Watch what happens when I breathe on this mirror. Did you ever use your finger to write or draw on a car window? How did your finger feel? What was the weather like outside?"

Get Concrete. By getting more hands-on, minds-on experience, children can tackle a concept that otherwise would prove too difficult. A third-grade teacher found that, although many of her students struggled with division, they could get the concept through a game where they were asked how many trips a toy truck would need to make across the bridge and over the river to transport various numbers of toy cars. The car transport problems were written on laminated cards and, after the children filled in the results, they could flip the card over to see the division fact.

Practice Together. When children are expected to complete a complex task independently, it is often helpful to do an example together first. The nature of that example is important. If the example does not transfer well to the group or independent activity, then the children will be confused when they have to do the individual task. A kindergarten teacher who was trying to explain the idea of sequence, for example, found that wordless books were an excellent way to provide a scaffold for story plot and that, by writing a group story to accompany one set of pictures in a wordless book, individual children could choose a wordless book and dictate or write an accompanying story.

Color Code and Highlight. The human brain tends to respond to powerful visual images (Rushton & Larkin, 2001). A teacher who wants to draw children's attention to something might consider using bright colors, such as a fluorescent pink card for the new letters that are being added to the rime (word family) of "–an." In teaching parts of speech, a teacher can construct sentences in which all of the nouns are red, and all of the verbs, blue. One also can buy rolls of removable, temporary adhesive highlighting tape in various thicknesses to highlight words in a big book or on a page of text (www.crystalspringsbooks.com).

Act It Out. Particularly where complex procedures are involved, dramatization can prove much more effective than verbal instruction. A lesson on school bus safety for kindergarten students used rows of chairs to represent seats on the bus. Some children pretended to be passengers while others were the audience. The teacher whispered various inappropriate behaviors (e.g., standing on the seat) and appropriate behaviors (e.g., looking both ways while exiting the bus), while the audience passed judgment on what was safe or unsafe behavior.

Toss It Out. Sometimes those who publish instructional materials suggest activities that are not well suited to children's developmental levels. A kindergarten lesson from a teachers' manual included a lesson on syllables in which children were expected to decide which syllable of the word was stressed. The teachers concluded that it would be more reasonable with this age group to make children aware of syllables through chants, raps, finger plays, and action rhymes.

Allow Mistakes. Although we may say that we learn from mistakes, most of us prefer to avoid them. In Reggie Routman's (1995) book, *Invitations*, she includes worksheets she refers to as "Have-a-Go" where children know they will not be evaluated and are asked to simply give a learning task a try as a starting point. Another teacher encouraged children to use DK to mean "don't know" as an alternative to just guessing. That way, he could scan their papers quickly and get a sense of what was perplexing to his students.

understanding are numerous. Although the example here does not make any claim to being a lesson meeting in the Japanese interpretation, it does offer some of the benefits identified by Lewis (2000), including:

- Individual professional development
- Learning to really see children
- Spreading new content and approaches
- Connecting individual teachers' practices to school goals and broader goals
- Allowing competing views of teaching to bump into one another
- Creating demand for improvement
- Honoring the central role of teaching

Using formal educational experiences at colleges and universities as the vehicle for improving teacher planning makes sense for several reasons. First of all, slightly over half of U.S. teachers will earn a master's degree, and virtually all states require some form of ongoing professional training. Concentrating on lesson planning in these venues diminishes the risk of exposing one's vulnerabilities to coworkers, something that might be problematic in schools. It also provides teachers with time to think and incentives to reteach, while making the course content more relevant and practical. In addition, structured professional development experiences give teachers the time to participate in collaborative planning—time that is in short supply in schools. Those who are responsible for planning professional development activities in basic education often take the approach of bringing in experts to give speeches and conduct workshops, evidently fearing that if teachers are given time to talk, it will deteriorate into gossip or grousing. Meetings that have as their goal the improvement of plans and teaching tend to avoid unfocused talk as they communicate respect for local expertise.

CONCLUSION: THE USEFUL DISTINCTION BETWEEN PERFORMANCE AND COMPETENCE

One of the distinctive things about the teaching profession is that most people in the United States have amassed at least 13 years, K–12, observing teacher behavior from a student's perspective. There is no other occupation that supplies so many real, live opportunities to observe as an assortment of people strive to fulfill a professional role. The breadth and depth of this experience often overrides teacher preparation experience, and it is not unusual for teachers under pressure to revert to what they experienced as children themselves rather than draw upon their professional training as the primary source for ideas (Whitbeck, 2000). A student teacher in first grade creates a construction paper "bookworm" consisting of a series of construction paper circles that record each child's independent reading choices. When asked where she got this idea, she replies, "I remember doing this when I was in first grade." A secondary biology teacher orders frogs to be dissected, an assignment that clearly is at odds with his conservationist stance on other issues. Yet it is not until a few students challenge the practice that it gives him great pause and he reconsiders the activity, which was an echo of his days as a high school biology student. Professors, called upon to teach methods courses, often do no better. They may revert to the brand of lesson planning they experienced years earlier, although now the demand to teach to higher standards renders much of that material useless or ineffectual.

When teachers assemble their portfolios, lessons and units are categorized as artifacts, a term borrowed from archaeology. Many, if not most, of those plans bear the markings of what went on long before in schools rather than what needs to occur today. As we will argue throughout the remainder of this book, a lesson plan should not be a curious relic from the field's past that serves to perpetuate outmoded ways of thinking and being in classrooms. The archaeologist turns to artifacts neither to guide current behavior nor to direct it into the future. Rather, such "finds" tell the story of what went on before, deepening insights into other cultures and eras. This should be no less true for that educational artifact we call the lesson plan. Planning must not be an occasion to thoughtlessly replicate what went on before in the name of teaching. Rather, planning must become a means of enlightenment that improves learning for students, enhances professional growth for educators, and forges bonds with diverse families and communities.

CHAPTER 2

Planning Together: Prospects and Barriers

Mr. Seton considers himself to be a successful science teacher, although he wishes his students' end-of-year test scores had been higher. He is most proud of his youthful, energetic approach to teaching; the interesting activities he finds on the Internet; the broad topic coverage he accomplishes each year; and, above all, the fact that his students are kept occupied so that behavior problems are minimized. Most of the curriculum materials used in Mr. Seton's class are from the textbook or accompanying supplementary materials. After 3 years of experience as a biology teacher, he was awarded tenure.

In the spring, he was notified of his transfer to another high school in his district. He is pleased to be moving because the students at this school are reputedly "easier" to teach—maybe this will be the answer to his students' rather disappointing test scores. At the school's annual farewell banquet, his principal wished him well and, pulling him aside, recommended that he spend more time planning and making the connection between curriculum and instruction in his new setting. "Wonder what she meant by that," he confides to a friend. "Students always looked forward to my class. It was fun. Students loved dissecting specimens and working on the computer."

It is fall and Mr. Seton enters his new classroom for the first time. The district provides three teacher workdays prior to the students' arrival, and the building is quiet except for occasional greetings exchanged between colleagues out in the hallway. As he sits at his desk, he considers what he might have done differently in his previous school—but not for long. His thoughts turn to the new crop of students that will appear in just 2 days' time, and as he begins thumbing through a worn teacher's manual, he feels a growing sense of anxiety about how he will handle six sections of Biology I during the first week of class.

41

Fortunately for Mr. Seton, a new colleague stops by to welcome him to the faculty and to invite him to the science department's planning session. Although reluctant to give up any of his dwindling time, in the spirit of collegiality, he joins her, not aware that his professional world is about to change forever. In this meeting of a dozen teachers, he finds that they, as a department, have aligned the curriculum to state standards, mapped topics and subject areas to avoid overlap and to fill gaps in instruction, and set up a system and schedule for all teachers of biology, chemistry, and physics to meet biweekly for common planning. In these meetings, he learns that his fellow biology teachers cooperatively set the subject map for each grading period, discuss resources, and share materials. Additionally, they review lesson plans to offer constructive advice to one another, and work to ensure that assessment strategies are reflective of the instruction and authentic, yet based on achieving state standards.

Mr. Seton is stunned—and awed. For the first time in his career, he understands the power and importance of planning for instruction. He also begins to realize how collaboration is far superior to his previous efforts to plan alone. Suddenly, the advice of his former principal begins to make sense, and he wonders how he could have taught for 3 years without the support of a teaching community.

PLANNING AS THE NUCLEUS OF EFFECTIVE TEACHING

EFFECTIVE PLANNING is an essential element of good teaching and of promoting student achievement. The planning process has a pervasive influence, as it applies to short-term and long-term planning and provides a framework to select goals; to develop activities and assignments that connect, expand, and extend identified knowledge, skills, and attitudes; and to design appropriate assessments that bring the planning process full circle. Effective planning makes learning purposeful and takes into consideration such disparate elements as setting objectives, the pacing of instruction, students' abilities, and resources needed. Mr. Seton's haphazard, last-minute approach to preparing for his Biology I class compromised his effectiveness and his students' overall achievement. Interestingly, he attributed any shortcomings in his teaching to the content, stating to a fellow teacher from his old school, "After all, teaching about the internal organs of invertebrates and vertebrates is not that exciting." He also failed—by emphasizing surfing the Internet, "fun," and superficial types of participation rather than problem finding, problem solving, and comprehensive performance assessment—to challenge students' intellects.

In many schools, teachers are held accountable for something they influence—student performance on standardized tests—but cannot be expected to control. Ironically, the task for which they should be held most accountable—effective lesson design, planning, and review—frequently is left to chance. "Because of the factory model that has dominated the thinking of the twentieth century, there is a tendency to think of improvement in terms of production—develop a design, reduce the process into sequential steps, and proceed from step to step until the finished product has been created" (DuFour & Eaker, 1998, p. 284). Effective planning, much like curriculum development, is a "means to an end, and not an end in itself" (English, 1992, p. ix). Recognizing these underlying assumptions can save the process.

Planning for instruction requires a personal/professional attitude that is characterized by a willingness to continually improve and strive for excellence. It forces one to relinquish familiar and comfortable methods of planning and teaching. In Goodlad's large-scale observational study, chronicled in *A Place Called School: Prospects for the Future* (1984), his overwhelming impression was that secondary schools are emotionally flat. Textbooks and teacher guides are complicit in this hidden curriculum of maintaining order above all else; English (1992) contends that even the textbooks have a decidedly deadening effect on children and that teachers become quite loyal to the content and ancillary materials. The array of products that accompany basic texts promote the false belief that effective planning has already been accomplished. The publisher's mantra is that these materials will save time. Because lesson design, planning, and review often are ignored or done in teachers' free time, the appeal of such materials is great. Likewise, activities on the Internet can beckon as a way to save (or fill) time. Ultimately, an uncritical dependence on such materials will undermine effectiveness and erode student achievement. When teachers surrender responsibility for lesson design and fail to reflect on their teaching, instruction becomes directionless and efficacy is compromised.

PLANNING WITH PURPOSE

Planning is as important in the classroom as it is in other areas of life. "Skill in planning is acknowledged to be one of the most influential factors in successful teaching" (Hunter, 1994, p. 87), and the vast majority of teachers, elementary and secondary, *do* engage in some form of instructional planning (McCutcheon & Milner, 2002; Sardo-Brown, 1990). The act of planning instruction for student achievement is such a remarkably simple concept, yet it often is ignored, underutilized, misinterpreted, or poorly executed.

One of the simplest, yet most powerful, avenues for effective planning is available to almost every teacher. It is what Mr. Seton discovered quite by accident—collaborative planning. Considering the case built for the importance of planning in and of itself, collaborative planning adds synergy to the process of lesson design and review. Planning collaboratively can be defined and practiced in such ways that it meets the needs of the teachers engaged in it. Teachers may see the need to plan with other grade-level teachers, subject-area teachers, and specialty teachers, such as art, music, or technology. Other options may include, but are certainly not limited to, planning instruction for day-to-day purposes, thematic units, special events, or simply to strengthen existing lessons. The key to collaborative planning is that there is strength in numbers—who better to support and assist teachers in planning endeavors than another teacher or teachers?

According to Jacobsen, Eggen, and Kauchak (2006), there are four primary purposes for planning: conceptual, organizational, emotional, and reflective. Taking each in turn, we will pose possibilities for effective planning through a series of questions categorized by theme.

1. Conceptual

What knowledge, skills, or attitudes do teachers want students to learn? What conceptual decisions about goals and student learning need to be considered? What sequence of activities would best serve meeting learning goals? What types of assessments reflect the learnings achieved?

- Collaborative planning can help answer these questions by focusing on the conceptual reasons for planning. Identifying these is perhaps the most important consideration in the planning process, as it is baseline to all other elements of planning. Teacher planning groups can use the strategy of brainstorming at some times, and a "divide, conquer, and reconvene" method at other times. The opportunity to pool thoughts, collect ideas, and share experiences will likely expand and refine existing or developing lesson plans. Collaborative planning is the educator's version of the medical profession's holistic health care; it uses a panel of experts to provide a more comprehensive and precise diagnosis and treatment plan. Lesson plans that are designed, implemented, and evaluated by a group of teachers embody multiple perspectives that provide more meaningful, challenging, and connected instructional experience for students.

2. Organizational

What time and physical factors affect being able to implement the end results of planning? What budget is in place? Are materials available? What populations are served? What are the needs of the students?

- Collaborative planning can greatly improve teachers' knowledge as to what materials or resources already exist. It is not uncommon for teachers of the same subject or grade level to be unaware of what is available within the school for use in the classroom. Not only could instructional materials be inventoried, but the budget could be reviewed to avoid ordering unnecessary multiples of equipment or supplies. Furthermore, the unique needs of students in general, as well as of subpopulations, could be discussed to share what is known to ensure all identified needs are addressed.

3. Emotional

What confidence level exists when a teacher has done his or her "homework"? What content knowledge needs to be learned or refreshed? What level of anxiety exists when teachers know that they are underprepared?

- Collaborative planning provides a safety net for all involved. As Maslow's hierarchy of needs suggests, "belonging" precedes "self-actualization." Being a valued part of a group of professional educators encourages a productive work ethic and a sense of pride in individual and collective achievements. Stronger teachers will have a positive effect on less confident planners, who in turn will grow in their contributions to the group. Through collaborative planning, experienced teachers have a venue to contribute to the next generation of teachers as newcomers are socialized into the value of lesson design, delivery, and review.

4. Reflective

What can be learned from experience? What does or does not work? What can be done to strengthen one's teaching? Are there gaps or duplications in the curriculum that need to be addressed?

- Although teachers can reflect on instruction at any point in time, reflecting upon one's teaching immediately after the experience, while the experience is fresh, has distinct benefits. Debriefing with others provides a forum for teachers to share their instructional successes and failures, student reactions, problems encountered, objectives achieved, and any digressions from the planned instruction. Engaging in this process affords teachers an on-the-spot opportunity to adjust the lesson plan for future use in order to reteach the lesson with those modifications in place. Insights about what proved more effective can then be applied to other lessons and planning, all with an eye toward the "3Es"—effectiveness, efficacy, and efficiency (Friedland & Walz, 2003).

THE CASE FOR COLLABORATIVE PLANNING

Teacher self-evaluation is a continuous process that occurs before, during, and after instruction and may take various forms as teachers engage in reflective self-talk about their actions in the classroom, such as:

- "I didn't allow enough time for this lesson," or, conversely, "I allowed too much time for this. What am I going to do for the remainder of the afternoon?"
- "This activity is going well. My students have made connections with the topic," or, conversely, "What was I thinking? They appear to be enjoying the activity, but I do not believe I am really getting my key points across."
- "I am proud of the work students are producing for this culminating activity," or, conversely, "I never imagined that we'd need so many materials to construct these models. I am disappointed in the outcome."

These are examples of "on-the-spot" reflections. In some cases, planning mistakes are salvageable; in others, they are not. Reflection on instruction enables teachers to learn from their mistakes.

Evaluation, too, is an important element in the planning process. It is through assessment efforts that the teacher more fully understands what actually was learned. Careful review of the results, whether the assessments are informal and formative in nature or are formal and summative, gives teachers a great deal of information as to how to proceed instructionally from that point.

School environments where there are no universal, explicit sets of goals for student achievement are common (Stigler & Hiebert, 1999). Teachers are often left to their own devices to determine goals, methods, and assessments for their students; this is more likely to occur in schools where individual planning is the norm. Imagine, if you will, a wagon drawn by four horses. The horses, strong and capable, are not all hitched to the front of the wagon. Rather, a horse is hitched to each side of the wagon—four horses, four sides—all pulling and straining to move the cart in different directions—an impossible situation if the goal is to move forward. Teaching without active collaborative planning mirrors this image, and student achievement suffers. On the other hand, schools in which teachers plan collaboratively can better identify goals, thoughtfully discuss the culture and philosophy of the school, and make the corrections necessary to pull together with the same destination in mind.

Many colleges of education teach strategies of decades past. Contrary to what many undergraduate preservice teachers or, for that matter, practicing teachers might think, planning is not limited to lessons on paper. There are many important planning functions that are barely touched upon in the traditional, linear plan, such as establishing the physical and social environment of the classroom; adapting curriculum to student and teacher needs; developing unit, weekly, or daily lesson plans; preparing elements of the interactive processes of instruction; considering appropriate instructional strategies; locating materials and resources; or establishing routines and procedures in the classroom (Clark & Peterson, 1986).

Part of moving toward effective lesson design, delivery, and review is understanding how practitioners plan in the absence of opportunities for collaborative planning. As mentioned in Chapter 1 (Sardo-Brown, 1990), practicing teachers do not credit their preservice planning instruction with influencing how they plan for instruction or make instructional decisions in their own classrooms. This rift between lesson planning as it is taught in many colleges of education and lesson planning as it is practiced in the classroom calls upon teacher educators to depart from routine and widely practiced methods of instruction (Yinger & Nolan, 2003). If teachers are much more likely to formulate mental images (Ornstein, 1997) to guide planning rather than to devise extensive written plans, then preservice teachers need practice tools for visualizing lessons and curriculum, such as maps and webs. If teacher planning tends to be idiosyncratic, responsive to the task at hand, and is a form of mental rehearsal (McCutcheon & Milner, 2002; Sardo-Brown, 1990), then the challenge for teacher educators is to make experienced teachers' exemplary lesson planning processes visible to novices. In Gose's (2004) investigation of "curriculum animation," defined as how to bring curriculum to life, teacher curriculum planning was found to be informal, intuitive, and organic. Teachers frequently noted that they trusted their intuition, and one teacher commented that there is simply no linear, logical way to go about the process.

With this in mind, the format of plans so zealously taught in cook-book fashion bears reevaluation. At the very least, the lesson plan, as most educators know it, will have to become more flexible and fluid. Writing a traditional linear plan is comparable to voice exercises for a vocalist, while the master teacher's plan is the equivalent of a polished performance on stage.

Despite the best intentions of politicians, the general public, and educators themselves, the bottom line of improving students' achievement rests on the quality of the teacher and the quality of the teaching. A *qualified* teacher may or may not be a *quality* teacher (Wise & Darling-Hammond, 1995). Despite many attempts at regulating schools, including management designs, standardized tests, and national and state standards, student learning simply cannot be "teacher-proofed" (Darling-Hammond, 2003b). That is to say, developing a rigid, lockstep instructional package is not possible, nor is it desirable when educational systems contemplate the enormity of the task expected of them. Due to the intricacies of teaching and the staggering challenges faced by schools today, it is apparent that there is no single focus or methodology that will solve all student achievement problems. As Wiggins (2003) observed, U.S. students are the most tested and the least examined students in the world. Advances in student achievement hinge on rethinking and reinventing actions regarding planning, as well as what is done to implement instruction and to assess what has or has not been learned. Students have the capacity and interest to learn. Reacting to the assertions made by Hiebert and Stigler (2000) that "the concept of schools [being] places for teachers to learn is nearly foreign in American education" (p. 14), we contend that schools *can* be learning places for teachers, which requires "planning to plan."

Vision and commitment, according to Ayers (2001), are the bedrock of effective teaching. The same could be said of collaborative planning, for it is the time and place to share vision and forge a commitment. By its nature and definition, collaborative planning involves multiple perspectives and enables teachers to engage in "deep talk as knowing" (Himley, 1991) about teaching. As they participate in professional communities dedicated to improving instruction, teachers become students of teaching. Interaction with colleagues reminds teachers of the reasons they first chose teaching as a profession and affirms the professional obligations of the job. Teachers are ultimately responsible for their own performance in the classroom, but planning collaboratively focuses squarely on professional practice and in so doing reestablishes a vision of what teaching can and should be. Despite this, certain factors conspire to thwart teachers from planning collaboratively.

RECOGNIZING AND SURMOUNTING
BARRIERS TO COLLABORATIVE PLANNING

What teachers do or do not do to prepare for instruction influences the quality of the planning process and the results of that planning. Collaborative planning can improve teachers' planning processes by enhancing opportunities to learn from experience, by focusing on curriculum development, and by recognizing and overcoming obstacles to achieving mastery. However, eight barriers impede—or at least complicate—the quest for more effective planning.

Barrier 1: Teaching in Isolation

> Janet loves her teaching job, but she finds planning for three different preps to be exasperating. She commented to her colleague, Ed, that she felt like a mouse on its exercise wheel—a great deal of effort, but she simply wasn't getting anywhere. Ed invited her to join him during his planning period, as he was teaching two of the same classes. With a great sigh of relief, she accepted his kind offer.

In 1983, Clark described planning as an invisible and solitary part of teaching. Almost a quarter of a century later, this observation still applies to the planning process as it is experienced by most U.S. teachers. In schools in the United States, founded on capitalism and enamored with a philosophy of "rugged individualism," this isolation is considered a normal and acceptable work environment in schools. It may be the typical planning mode for classroom instruction, but it is an unnecessary burden teacher educators and classroom teachers bear. There is a point of friction between being completely autonomous, or perhaps even competitive, in our work, and conversely, functioning as a team member dedicated to collaboration, sharing, and the best interests of students for better results.

In most American public schools, opportunities to see other teachers in action are rare (Wasley, 1999), collegial feedback is almost nonexistent, and occasions to learn new instructional strategies are limited at best. These circumstances are daunting for seasoned, experienced teachers, but can be devastating to the novice teacher who struggles to survive the rigors of his or her new profession. Complicating feelings of insecurity are misconceptions novices may have regarding the planning process in general and specifically collaborative planning. When a group of preservice teachers who have just begun to learn how to write lesson plans and engage in classroom observation were queried, the following responses were given:

- "Planning is a good idea because it solves many problems before they occur."
- "A good teacher must be prepared emotionally and organizationally."
- "The biggest problem I face is shoving three or four ideas into one plan. I also have a hard time having the whole lesson focused on one key idea."
- "Making a lesson fun is my main goal."

Regarding collaborative planning, preservice teachers remarked:

- "Collaborative planning can be a problem because of an unequal workload."
- "I know when I first enter the teaching field, I will want to work with someone more experienced so I know how they like to do things."
- "Collaborative planning makes me less afraid of failure."

It is clear that these comments identify some of the planning difficulties that will challenge the soon-to-be newest in our ranks. The planning process itself gets off to a faulty start almost before it begins. Teacher isolation gives novices a frightening sense of being the first and only ones to have charted the territory. There is no systemic provision for sharing what we know—and seemingly a limited desire to do so.

Isolation also affects experienced teachers, who may lament the fact that "we never have the chance to see one another teach or to talk about what we are doing." In a culture that rewards individual striving, teachers can be just as reluctant to share their best work as they are to discuss their shortcomings. As one teacher stated, "I did a lot of work on this project, and my grade-level group never does anything creative. Why should I give them all of my work to copy?" Collaborative planning addresses such concerns by setting a consistent expectation of positive and strong contributions by all teachers in service to all students.

Barrier 2: Experience Lost

Russell, an experienced teacher of 5 years, feels worn out from his planning efforts. He doesn't understand why his department has nothing available to assist him in efforts to plan exciting, thought-provoking lessons. "I could write a book on this myself," he thought, "if only I had the time." "My cousin is a doctor," he mentioned to his principal. "Whenever he gets stumped, he consults his medical journals. . . ." As his voice trailed off, he brightened up and said, "I hate to be uninformed, but does our school have a professional section in the library for teachers?"

It is the rare teacher who records what was learned about lesson design, planning, or review. Educators retire or exit the profession leaving their replacements to begin anew (Stigler & Hiebert, 1999). This is in stark contrast to the practice in Japan and Taiwan, where a concerted and systematic effort is made "to pass on the accumulated wisdom of teaching practice to each new generation of teachers and to keep perfecting that practice by providing teachers the opportunities to continually learn from each other" (Stigler & Stevenson, 1991, p. 46). Imagine what would result if other professionals, such as physicians, attorneys, or architects, conducted their work without consultation.

Collaborative planning results in written lessons that accumulate and contribute to the wisdom of the field. A compelling illustration of this can be seen in a small, rural school district in the northeast. Two years of experience with collaborative planning has brought one group of middle and high school teachers to a place where they focus on a broad topic tied to district goals. Each member of this group of eight teachers is responsible for selecting an instructional strategy related to the topic and for presenting it to the group, much like a presentation at a professional conference. Each presentation is designed to instruct and inform the others in the group and is open to discussion regarding the pros and cons of the strategy presented. Upon completion, each presenter compiles instructional materials into a three-ring binder so that group members can revisit the materials, raise questions, or seek assistance.

Barrier 3: Research Denied

Attitudes about the conduct and use of research vary in schools. According to Cochran-Smith and Lytle (1993):

> Teachers are . . . expected to be the eventual recipients of the knowledge generated by professional researchers. That is, they are expected to acknowledge the value of researchers' work for their own professional practice and to accept its validity for their day-to-day decisions. Consequently, beginning as well as in-service teacher education programs are typically organized to disseminate a knowledge base constructed almost exclusively by outside experts. (p. 1)

Research, however, need not come exclusively from outside experts. The field of action research, where teachers reflect upon their own practice and engage in inquiry, is growing. The notion of claiming or reclaiming ownership for one's own professional development is not a new one, but one that provides an opportunity for a fresh look for teachers to identify research interests, establish guidelines for research planning, and contemplate the role of reflection in conducting research (Burnaford, Fischer, & Hobson, 2001). Teachers who involve themselves with inquiry in their own classrooms position themselves to better understand the value of research conducted in the larger context of outside experts. These teachers are more likely to accept and use this research in their own practice.

However, at least some practices that pass as research-based are, in actuality, instructional myths, based on what Vaughn and Linan-Thompson (2004) call "folklore" or "craft." *Folklore* includes things that are passed from teacher to teacher, year to year, and generation to generation. Examples include, "Always teach reading in the morning," or "Have three reading groups." Folklore may contain a grain of truth and therefore have intuitive appeal, but it is not particularly helpful where viable professional growth is the goal.

Craft, on the other hand, implies those skills or areas of knowledge that are learned by trial and error. This level of functioning may be on a slightly higher plane than folklore, but trial and error is a very inefficient form of learning that often is accompanied by a large measure of frustration on the learner's part. Craft relegates education to the "semiprofessional" category and typically results in little more than a set of skills followed in an invariant sequence.

Folklore and craft dominate habits of planning and make educational research a casualty in the lesson design, delivery, and review process. As one highly regarded teacher in a Virginia elementary school remarked,

> Research? Are you kidding me? When do I have the time to read research? What do those people in the Ivory Tower know about what I need or what my daily life is in my classroom? When was the last time they were in the classroom? In a perfect world, I am sure research would be great!

Cochran-Smith and Lytle (1993) note that the reputation of educational research is in and of itself an obstacle to teachers engaging in and benefiting from an inquiry stance on teaching. Teachers may look upon research with suspicion, or even contempt, when their failure to use evidence-based methods is blamed for past educational failures. "To many teachers, research is more or less by definition something that is distant, uninteresting, and impenetrable" (p. 89).

Collaborative planning can address this issue by strengthening the curriculum, instruction, and assessment trilogy through forging stronger linkages among theory, research, and professional practice. This bond is exemplified by a fifth-grade teacher who works collaboratively with a gifted education teacher. Both enthusiastically report that their rural district supports and encourages collaborative planning. In fact, it is an option that teachers may select to satisfy their district-wide professional development requirement. These teachers decided to work as partners to strengthen grade-level language arts instruction, especially as it applies to diversity issues and assessment in their guided reading program. They meet "semi-regularly" when parent or committee meetings do not usurp their time for this activity. Reflecting on the value of their collaboration, they note that other teachers contribute to their efforts and that they collaborate outside of their group of two. In other words, the synergy of their pairing extends beyond themselves and has influenced the formation of other informal collaborative alliances.

Barrier 4: Curriculum Conundrum

> "What exactly is my curriculum?" Pamela, who is new to her school, asked another teacher. "I have my textbook and the materials that came with our new adoption. I also have a binder in my closet that says 'Language Arts for the New Decade—1980.'" "Oh no," her friend responded. "We aligned the curriculum last spring. You should have received one in your mailbox on your first day here. But no matter, you can have mine; I have never even cracked the cover on it."

Many public schools store curriculum guides that are unused, unwanted, out-of-date, or simply too ponderous for most teachers to cull from. Collaborative lesson planning can bring key curricular components into alignment—an important step in improving instructional effectiveness—and close the gap between the written, taught, and tested curriculum (English, 1992). Every school needs a curriculum that is "guaranteed and viable." Marzano (2003) defines "guaranteed" not in the classic sense of certainty, but as a combination of conditions where every child has not only the time but also the opportunity to learn. Action steps toward developing a "guaranteed and viable" curriculum can become a code of practice for curriculum development for teachers as they inaugurate collaborative instructional planning. A synopsis of each consideration is offered as follows:

1. Identify content considered essential for students to learn. With curricula being filled to the point of overflowing in an attempt to meet all kinds of student needs, it is rare to see a core curriculum identified and communicated to all stakeholders. (p. 25)

2. Pair identified essential content with the amount of time that is
    necessary to teach the material. (p. 29)
3. Order the curriculum in a logical and sequential fashion to maximize
    learning potential. (p. 30)
4. Avoid idiosyncratic curriculum decisions. Administrators can support
    collaborative curriculum and instructional processes by ensuring that
    teachers do indeed address the essential content. (p. 30)
5. Protect the instructional time that is available. It is one thing to designate
    time to teach a particular part of the curriculum; it can be quite another
    to protect the allotted time treating it like the sacred commodity that it is.
    (p. 31)

Unless and until these steps can be embraced and enacted, preferably in
collaboration with others, planning will fail to fulfill its role as a route to
enhanced learning opportunities for students.

Barrier 5: Structural Paucity

Without the requisite structural supports, collaborative planning is un-
likely to flourish. Visions of what collaborative planning could be—and
should be—may be driven administratively or by teachers, or preferably
by both. All types of journeys have a destination and some sort of plan for
arriving there; teaching is no exception. Heidi Hayes Jacobs (1997) makes
the following analogy between seafaring and curriculum planning:

> Navigators use maps to chart a course. Although unforeseen events and
> variables may affect their journey, they begin by making important choices
> about their route to avoid a meandering, rudderless voyage. In similar
> fashion, teachers must make critical choices as they plot a course for their
> learners. (p. 25)

An example of a district that is trying to encourage collaborative planning is highlighted by Samantha, an urban grade 5 middle school teacher.

> My school district encourages collaborative planning in some re-
> spects. What I have seen in the primary grades is an attempt to col-
> laboratively plan, but the results are that the specific building may
> do the same things, but collaborative efforts change from building
> to building. At my grade level, and throughout the district, we have
> been asked to get together to develop ten "power standards" for
> classroom teachers to use as guidelines to teach several curricula.
> Despite frustrations and certain elements of disorganization, I think
> that the key is to keep the big picture in mind, the students. I feel

this collaborative process has definitely aided in receiving higher test scores and in planning in general. More effort is needed to smooth the process out, but it has helped.

As is seen here, the district has the right idea, but the element of floundering is clearly present. If other, failed educational efforts are taken into consideration, when teachers do not see the fruits of their individual or collective labor, initiatives often fade and are branded a failure. Another example of structural weakness can be illustrated by Katie, a high school teacher of 11th-grade English. She commented that her school's attempts with collaborative planning could best be described as *collaboration in absentia*. "Collaboration broke down because nobody seemed to know what the others were doing, and some of them didn't even know what *they* were supposed to be doing." She further noted that follow-through was sometimes lacking. For example, the group agreed to create an English department resource center to be housed in the faculty planning room:

> Rather than go door-to-door begging for good ideas, we decided that it would be easier for experienced and new teachers to have access to the cream of the crop at any time. We started last year with one unit and filed our ideas and strategies according to the state standards. When we returned this fall, a new wave of building-level initiatives hit us, and we lost momentum for our resource center. People are still sharing ideas, but we are back to the door-to-door approach.

As this example illustrates, administrative support is a scaffold on which more effective planning can be built. In the absence of such structure, collaborative planning often fails to thrive.

Barrier 6: Lack of Planning Time

> Joaquin, a teacher of 9 years, is desperately behind in his planning and grading. His planning period today was used to cover the class of a colleague who became ill and needed to leave school. With teaching new classes this year, even after teaching for 9 years, Joaquin has no files from which to draw ideas. Despite his broad background in mathematics content, he is often at a loss about the pedagogical aspects of math, so he refers to the teaching manuals and sketches an outline of the next chapter for each course. His last waking thought is, "That's it! I'll ask the students to fill in a blank outline. I hope they don't realize that I am assigning this just to fill time."

Time is always at a premium when it comes to the planning of instruction. This applies to individual planning as well as collaborative planning; however, collaborative planning is typically prearranged and more time-efficient, as it pools the intellect, experience, and resources of multiple professionals. Even though teachers are provided with mandated planning periods during the instructional week and sporadic days designated for professional development during the course of the school year, it is never enough time to achieve the level of instructional expertise demanded in today's schools. Collaborative planning could have alleviated the stress of Joaquin's situation of being new to his subject matter. His haphazard lesson plan, devised in desperation, would have been replaced by a lesson that a group of teachers designed in advance, thus bolstering Joaquin's confidence and resulting in a better learning experience for his students.

Collaborative planning not only builds teachers' willingness to try new ideas, but also provides support if these new ideas fall short of original expectations. Covering material takes very little planning; uncovering material through critical-thinking strategies takes a great deal of intellectual rigor on the part of the classroom teacher.

In the absence of reflection and lesson review by respected colleagues, even experienced teachers can succumb to what Sizer and Sizer (1999) call bluffing. Bluffing is a form of false confidence created by comparing oneself with the worst level of performance with a statement such as, "A poor plan must be superior to no plan." Bluffing also leads to self-deception with rationalizations such as, "I'm sufficiently experienced as a teacher to make up my plans as I go along." Teachers often may resort to bluffing in response to time constraints when the superficial has become accepted practice in particular school contexts. Preservice teachers, too, struggle with time for planning. Although understanding and generating lesson plans is a necessary teaching tool, many preservice teachers have long regarded the lengthy, linear plans produced in isolation as tedious and unnecessary (Lederman & Niess, 2000). They could be right. There is more to be gained through thoughtful dialogue about an array of plans on a topic gleaned from online sources (see the Appendix) than from a lone student's attempt to produce an original lesson plan. When novices are assigned to collect and critique the published plans of other teachers, technology becomes a way of simulating interaction with more experienced educators. Figure 2.1 is an example of an assignment for teacher education students that promotes collaboration via technology. For more on telementoring, see Abbott (2003).

Figure 2.1 Using Technology to Collaborate with Experienced Teachers

Instructions: Now that you know your grade-level assignment for your practicum and have identified several themes or units that will be taught during your field experience, your assignment is to gather resources to support four of these units/themes.

1. Begin by online searching a grade level, subject area (e.g., science, reading/language arts), and topic (e.g., magnets, writing a persuasive paragraph). Check several different sites for each theme or unit.
2. Analyze the resources and plans. What objectives, materials, activities, and procedures would you select for use with your students and what would you reject? Why? What ideas do you have and how will you combine them with what you found online?
3. Create a compendium of resources for each unit/theme. You need three types of information:

    • A set of general teaching goals with supporting online sources and their URLs.
    • Print resources to support the theme/unit.
    • Children's books related to the unit/theme.

Example: The following is a collection to support a first-grade theme on pets, organized by teaching goals. This is just like what you are to produce for each of your four themes/units.

Teaching Goals and Online Resources to Support Them

1. To expand children's knowledge of animals and related vocabulary
NAEYC Learning Continuum Indicator 1.1.F, Learning to Read Independently, Understanding new vocabulary learned in various subjects.

    • Animal sounds. Learn about animal sounds and how they are represented in different languages: www.georgetown.edu/faculty/ballc/animals/animals.html
    • Pets Rock! Get facts about pets around the world: http://www.kn.sbc.com/wired/fil/pages/listpetser.html

2. To develop research and writing skills
NAEYC Learning Continuum Indicator 1.4.B, Types of Writing, Write informational sentences.

    • Research different animals: www.enchantedlearning.com/themes/pets.html
    • Make an electronic scrapbook of a pet: http://www.kn.sbc.com/wired/fil/pages/scrapcaringfce.html

3. To inspire creativity and make connections with the arts
NAEYC Learning Continuum Indicator 1.6.F, Speaking and Listening, Using elec-
tronic media for learning purposes, such as generating a journal or a story.

- Neopets. Invent a habitat for a virtual pet: www.neopets.com
- Education Place. Create a schedule for a pet: http://www.eduplace.com/
  cgi-bin/searchengine.cgi
- Make a creature collage: http://www.eduplace.com/activity/1_6_act1.
  html

4. To promote humane education
NAEYC Learning Continuum Indicator 1.6.A, Listens to others when they are
speaking to demonstrate understanding of the message.

"A process that encourages an understanding of the need for compassion
and respect for people, animals and the environment and recognizes the
interdependence of all living things" (www.worldanimal.net).

- The Society for the Prevention of Cruelty to Animals (SPCA) (http://
  www.aspca.org) has several curriculum kits suitable for young children.
- Humane Education Programs: http://www.humaneedu.com
- The Latham Foundation: www.latham.org

5. To teach children to stay safe around animals
NAEYC Learning Continuum Indicator 1.6.B, Speaking and Listening, Asking
questions to obtain clarifying information.

The Humane Society and the National Association for Humane and Environmental Education (NAHEE) (http://www.nahee.org/) offer a curriculum kit suitable for
preschool through third grade that includes a video ("Bow Wow Ow!"), puppets, a
BINGO game, a poster, and other resources. To see a sample lesson plan, visit http://
www.nevadacf.org/dogbitelesson2.pdf. In addition, NAHEE offers the *BARK Dog Bite
Prevention Program* for elementary school children, with a coloring book and video,
and the *Kind News* newsletter for children.

- Love Your Dog (http://www.loveyourdog.com) offers advice on responsible pet ownership and "Keeping Safe: Don't Bother Dogs," a list of
  seven basic rules, illustrated with photographs, that help to prevent dog
  bites. The materials are suitable for K–3.
- Doggone Safe (http://www.doggonesafe.com) includes a free 3.5-minute
  "Learn to Speak Dog" video that teachers can use to help children cor-
  rectly interpret the behavior of dogs. The video uses live footage of dogs,
  rather than cartoons, to teach children to read dog body language, and
  emphasizes responsible pet keeping.
- Treasured Pets—presents a series of questions to be answered to determine which pets are appropriate. http://www.kn.sbc.com/wired/fil/
  pages/huntpetsr.html

Online Sources Consulted:

Gateway to Educational Materials: A portal to thousands of lesson plans; just type "pets" in the search box: www.thegateway.org

Filamentality: A link to thousands of pet theme activities: www.kn.pacbell.com/wired/fil

Pet Quest: Decide whether to get a classroom pet and, if so, which one: http://www.kn.sbc.com/wired/fil/pages/webpetquesal.html

The American Society for the Prevention of Cruelty to Animals —AnimaLessons: http://www.aspca.org/site/PageServer?pagename=al_home

The Role of Children's Literature in Humane and Environmental Education Programs. (Annotated Bibliography—compiled February 2005): http://www.savemoreanimals.org/humane/online.pdf

Print Resources

Barker, S. B., Rogers, C. S., Turner, J. W., Karpf, A. S., & Suthers-Mccabe, H. M. (2003). Benefits of interacting with companion animals: A bibliography of articles published in refereed journals during the past 5 years. *American Behavioral Scientist, 47*(1), 94–99.

Jalongo, M. R. (2004). *The world's children and their companion animals: Developmental and educational significance of the child/pet bond.* Olney, MD: Association for Childhood Education International.

Jalongo, M. R. (2005). Implementing a reading education assistance dog program. *Childhood Education, 81*(3), 153–156.

Larson, J. (2002) Be kind to animals. *Book Links, 12*(2), 15–17.

Melson, G. F. (2003). Child development and the human–companion animal bond. *American Behavioral Scientist, 47*(1), 31–39.

Raphael, P., Coleman, L., & Loar, L. (1999). *Teaching compassion: A guide for humane educators, teachers, and parents.* Alameda, CA: Latham Foundation for the Promotion of Humane Education.

Rivera, M. A. (2004). *Canines in the classroom: Raising humane children through interactions with animals.* New York: Lantern Books.

Picture Books for Suitable for First Grade

Bubba and Beau, Best Friends (Appelt, 2002)

"Let's get a pup!" said Kate (Graham, 2001)

The Puppy Who Wanted a Boy (Thayer, 1988)

The Stray Dog (Simont, 2000)

Rosie, A Visiting Dog's Story (Calmenson, 1994)

What About My Goldfish? (Greenwood, 1993)

Madeline's Rescue (Bemelmans, 1953)

Archie, Follow Me (Cherry, 1990)

Dr. White (Goodall, 1999)

Mrs. Katz and Tush (Polacco, 1992)

Bow Wow Meow Meow: It's Rhyming Cats and Dogs (Florian, 2003)

Bad Dog, Bodger! (Ambercrombie, 2002)

The New Puppy (Anholt, 1994)

Pet Wash (Dodds, 2001)

Be Gentle! (Miller, 1997)

Doggie Dreams (Chapman, 2000)

Mr. Davies and the Baby (Voake, 1996)

My Pig Amarillo (Ichikawa, 2003)

Mapping Penny's World (Leedy, 2000)

Cookie's Week (Ward, 1994)

As Wiggins and McTighe (1998) point out:

> Historically, U.S. education has minimized the role of planning and design
> in teaching. The frenetic pace of daily school schedules, the demands of
> non-teaching duties, and the general block of time reserved for planning
> (within and beyond the teaching day), make it difficult for educators to en-
> gage in substantive curricular planning and design work, especially with
> colleagues. (p. 158)

Doug, an English instructor at an urban postsecondary art school, echoes
this concern as it applies to his planning, by saying, "lack of time [is] a primary impediment. . . . Experience and familiarity with the courses, their
competencies and objectives, as well as the material itself, is what I rely
upon to get me through."

In further conversation regarding issues related to planning time amid
other pressing responsibilities, he cites other colleagues who have "buck-
led under the pressure and sought work elsewhere." If schools expect
their teachers to plan effectively, adequate time to do so must be provided.
Innovative practices, such as the use of retreats or summer work groups,
may be particularly effective, as they segregate planning for a new venture from time so closely juxtaposed to teaching time (Cambone, 1995). It
is often difficult to infuse a new idea into a teacher's life during the school
year, because there are many competing demands on time and attention.
However, if an innovation such as collaborative planning is to take root,
regular, uninterrupted blocks of time must be provided.

Instituting collaborative planning is not without drawbacks, however.
One high school English teacher remarks that her school has a built-in, 45-
minute period designated as "common planning time." Its purpose is for
teachers at her grade level to meet together for the express purpose of collaborative planning. She shares, however, that school activities and meetings typically encumber this time and that true collaborative planning is
rare. Even the best intentions and the will to participate in collaborative
planning may yield to external pressures.

Barrier 7: Cultural Scripting

It is surprisingly easy to follow the scripts for teaching that have been
so amply observed by teachers and teacher educators as students. "Playing
school" (Metzger, 1993) can cause teachers to repeat results in learning experiences that are essentially the same as they have been for generations.

Stigler and Hiebert (1999) define "cultural scripting" as a process
"learned implicitly through observation and participation, and not by deliberate study" (p. 84).

> It is not hard to see where the scripts come from or why they are widely shared. A cultural script for teaching begins forming early, sometimes even before children get to school. Playing school is a favorite preschool game. As children move through twelve years and more of school, they form scripts for teaching. All of us probably could enter a classroom tomorrow and act like a teacher, because we all share this cultural script. In fact, one of the reasons classrooms run as smoothly as they do is that students and teachers have the same script in their heads: they know what to expect and what roles to play. (p. 87)

A common example of cultural scripting occurs when teachers plan and implement engaging and effective instructional activities, yet administer the traditional paper-and-pencil, multiple-choice test that denies students the opportunity to demonstrate application and mastery of skills. Colleagues who plan together are in a better position to note such schisms between instruction and assessment. Consider, for example, the sixth-grade teacher who crafts a lesson on the use of the microscope. The performance goal is for students to understand how to use the instrument by observing various prepared slides. The teacher supplies several "mystery" slides for students to speculate about what they see. However, the unit test consists of nothing more than a schematic drawing of a microscope on which students are asked to identify and label the primary parts.

Collaboration becomes a way of writing a new script, as all sixth-grade teachers in the building establish the goals and concepts of the unit on using microscopes; brainstorm a list of activities to accomplish the goals; narrow the list to the most compelling based on time, materials, and readiness of the students; and agree upon the most logical and efficacious means of assessment.

Barrier 8: Blaming Others

True professionals do not wait for their mistakes to become public knowledge or attempt to shift blame. They own up to their errors, vow to do better, and then actually do so, partly out of a desire to avoid letting others down and partly out of an obligation to develop as professionals (Jalongo, 2002). There is a reason why many states have instituted no-fault insurance and no-fault divorces; ascribing blame is unproductive, even counterproductive. Teachers' complaining about what was or was not taught at the middle school, griping about the way a principal conducts observations, or protesting that a child entered kindergarten not knowing her letters is important only with regard to steps that can be taken to improve the situation.

Part of cultural rescripting involves reflecting on and reframing questions (McEntee, Appleby, Dowd, Grant, Hole, & Silva, 2003), going from blame-focused questions such as, "What's wrong with students these days? I would never have been so disrespectful to my teachers!" to new questions over which teachers can exert some influence such as, "How can I do a better job of managing the classroom and troubleshooting the parts of a lesson that are apt to be difficult for students?" Collaborative planning, once again, would be a reasonable and expected venue for shifting the focus from blaming others to more introspective thoughts aimed at sorting out problems and concerns, deciding where the locus of control lies, and strategizing possible solutions.

THE ESSENTIALS OF COLLABORATIVE PLANNING: AN EXAMPLE

Identifying problems with the planning process is a relatively simple task; finding solutions is considerably more challenging. However, a number of purposes can prompt the use of collaborative planning, as illustrated by the desire and momentum created through the action of one teacher, John Richards.

> Mr. Richards is a social studies teacher at a suburban middle school. He proposes to his colleagues at the eighth-grade level that they design an interdisciplinary unit on human rights, a concept and constellation of issues that he feels strongly about and one that has been broached in a number of ways by his students. He envisioned the unit as requiring the expertise of social studies, mathematics, language arts, art, and science teachers.
>
> Mr. Richards was quite disappointed when his fellow teachers reacted with resistance to his idea. They were not accustomed to planning together and had very specific ideas regarding what should be taught at what time of year. They were experienced enough to be comfortable with individual planning, although a few admitted to feeling a bit stale with presenting the same material time and time again. One was intimidated by having to conduct Internet research, or any kind of research—"I haven't done any real research since I was in college," this teacher remarked. Another was reluctant to spend the time it takes to organize, discuss, and design a new curriculum. Two were fearful of offering any subject matter that was controversial—"You know how conservative this community is! I don't want parents on my doorstep." Ultimately, Mr. Richards's persistence and enthusiasm for the project prevailed and these five teachers began their first venture in collaborative planning.

They agreed that this instruction must be student-centered, thought-provoking, and, in the end, community-based. It also was decided that involving parents was a wise strategy, as this would keep everyone involved and a part of the project. Mr. Richards invited Mrs. Elliot to sit with him at his computer to see how user-friendly Internet research could be. They consulted Beane's *Curriculum Integration: Designing the Core of Democratic Education* (1997) to jump-start their efforts. As they began to get excited about their work, the issue of time melted away. They would use the time provided for planning at school wisely—and no one seemed any longer to mind scheduling additional sessions after school; after all, it was their choice to do so!

Those issues resolved, the group began to brainstorm the goals of this unit. They started with core questions: What is fair and what is not fair? What are the basic necessities of human dignity, safety, and freedom? What is the role of man-made laws with regard to social justice? They then brainstormed a list of activities that supported or expanded these questions. As their sessions proceeded, assessments were considered, including authentic activities, student writings, presentations, letters to the editor of the local newspaper, and a culminating community-based project.

A great deal of thought and consideration went into the planning of this unit, admittedly a new adventure for all teachers involved. Mr. Richards was correct in believing that this unit would be student-centered and engaging for his students. There are clearly interdisciplinary components included, and the introduction of human rights as a topic is in and of itself a powerful motivator for students and the teachers involved. However, simply because these teachers have spent many hours planning, there is absolutely no guarantee that these efforts will further student achievement, especially in those areas identified as important in the state curriculum. Many more hours will be spent implementing, assessing, and reflecting on this unit of instruction before any conclusions can be drawn. What is clear is that these teachers, planning collaboratively, are certainly on the right track in developing connected, meaningful, and engaging instruction. This portrayal of collaborative planning in action is analyzed in Figure 2.2.

The models of Marzano, Pickering, and Pollock (2001) and of Bredekamp and Rosegrant (1992) encourage the asking of provocative questions during the planning process, both individually and collaboratively. What is truly important for students to learn? How can teachers inspire the desire to learn? How active should teachers be in the learning process? Who commands the larger role in student learning—the teacher or the students? How can assessment be used as a learning tool?

Figure 2.2 Analysis of Collaborative Planning for a Unit on Human Rights

Learning Goals	Human Rights: Analysis of Collaborative Planning
Identification of Unit of Instruction: A need or requirement is defined	*What and How Instruction Is Chosen* • Topic of human rights selected by social studies teacher • Recognition that topic would require additional expertise • Student knowledge limited on this topic
Identification of Learning Objectives and Performance Indicators: Faculty needs; student-centered and engaging activities	*Faculty Skills Objectives* • Willingness to plan collaboratively • Technology skills *Student Skills Objectives* • Concept development • Involvement of family/community • Writing; presentations; activism; culminating project
Constructive Feedback: Used as a learning tool; provides additional opportunities for investigation and reinforcement	*Supporting Student Learning* • Focus on exploration, inquiry, and critical thinking • Cooperative learning • Infusion of creative arts, i.e., art, music, technology • Guided and independent practice • Opportunities to correct and re-create
Application and Evaluation: Using skills to solve problems or evaluating situations	*Utilizing Learning for Different Purposes* • *Application*: Focus on taking learning beyond the classroom, and/or in new applications or circumstances • *Problem Solving*: Analysis or evaluation of a situation

Adapted from Marzano, Pickering, & Pollock (2001) and Bredekamp & Rosegrant (1992)

The true beauty of learning a new and powerful teaching strategy—and collaborative planning is a prime example—is that it creates more questions than answers. But that is at the heart of the learning process, as teachers are unequivocally learners, too, as they practice the art and science of teaching.

CONCLUSION: TRANSFORMING THE PLANNING PROCESS

The act of planning is an essential ingredient in the overall effectiveness and value of the teaching process. As they plan together, teachers identify a preferred curricular destination, consult on ways to meet expectations for student achievement, and agree upon the most effective route to get them there. When teachers get on the same page curriculum-wise, new opportunities to enrich the classroom surface in the form of materials, community resources, and the like. In addition, collaborative planning is a critical strategy to make the most of whatever planning time is available, as several minds are wrapped around a problem in ways that may well elude a teacher/thinker working alone. The teacher who engages in collaborative planning is in a far better position to meet the challenges of today's classroom. Through collaboration, teachers can design instruction that provides students with the voice and choice necessary for full participation in a democratic society. Teacher learning becomes connected to student learning and provides teachers with the power, confidence, order, and purposefulness of instruction tied to a coherent, viable, and connected curriculum. Collaborative learning is more than a strategy of getting along with other teachers; it is a strategy for attaining excellence through engagement with other teachers in the planning process. Successful collaborative planning depends on the actions of teachers—their willingness and investment in this process—because school improvement is a human enterprise.

Lesson design, delivery, review, and redesign achieved collaboratively are essential to professionalism in teaching. We need only look at how other professions use collaboration to their benefit: The most mystifying medical conditions are addressed by teams of doctors; the highest-profile cases are handled by law firms; and the most heinous crimes are investigated by teams of detectives, psychologists, and crime scene investigators. There is little question that public education is being scrutinized and criticized as never before; second and third opinions—indeed a chorus of ideas—are warranted. Collaborative planning is a way to reclaim and refocus on education's primary mission—promoting student learning.

CHAPTER 3

Inaugurating Instructional Planning: The Education of Preservice and Novice Teachers

A s preservice and novice teachers think about planning, it is helpful to provide a questioning framework that serves as a tool for reflection on their roles as teachers. Over the years, we have asked the newest of the new teachers—those enrolled in their first methods courses—to consider questions such as these:

1. Why is it important for teachers to plan? What purposes does planning serve?
2. What problems have you encountered with lesson planning? What concerns do you have about planning for instruction?
3. How do you go about planning a lesson? Please do not describe what you believe you are *supposed* to do; rather, describe what you *actually* do. What do you typically do first and why? What do you do next? And so forth.
4. Please describe the best lesson that you have produced thus far. What made it special? Did you have an opportunity to teach the lesson? If so, what happened?
5. Is cooperative planning beneficial to preservice teachers? Why or why not?
6. What is your greatest concern about student teaching and how might planning together address that concern?

Some typical responses to these questions were:

"The best lesson I wrote was for a kindergarten classroom. We sang and learned the motions to a song. It was special because all of the children interacted and seemed to enjoy the lesson."

"In the plan, I first read a book that my teacher gave me. The book was about animals and their homes and I developed an activity to go along with the book. I had children create their own habitat using various materials. This was unique because it let the students be creative and yet met the standards."

"I wrote a lesson using music in creative writing. It was special because it was fun."

"I read a book that one of my former teachers had read about different types of clouds. The students put together binoculars, then went outside and looked at clouds. They created pictures with cotton balls. The children really enjoyed looking through binoculars at things around them."

In reviewing these comments from teacher education sophomores, two themes emerge: Lessons are good if they are "fun" for the students, and activities are "good" if they are endorsed by other teachers. Yet student teachers need to know not merely how to identify activities that students enjoy, or how to follow in the footsteps of former teacher educators, but how to attain teaching goals. First and foremost among those goals are improving student learning and furthering student achievement. In order to attain these goals, new teachers need to acquire five states of mind that support pupil development:

1. *Efficacy*—knowing that one has the capacity to make a difference and being willing and able to do so.
2. *Flexibility*—knowing one has, or can develop, options to consider; being willing to acknowledge and demonstrate respect for diverse perspectives.
3. *Craftsmanship*—seeking precision, refinement, and mastery.
4. *Consciousness*—monitoring one's own values, intentions, thoughts, and behaviors and their effect.
5. *Interdependence*—being committed to contribute to the common good and using group resources to enhance personal effectiveness (Adams, 2000b; Costa & Garmston, 1994; Garmston & Dyer, 1999).

Looking back to the students' comments, it is clear that the formidable task confronting teacher educators is to teach these five habits of mind to young, inexperienced prospective teachers. Through careful lesson planning, collaboration, and reflection, preservice teachers can enter the teaching force with the rudiments of efficacy, flexibility, craftsmanship, consciousness, and interdependence that lead to responsible colleagueship.

THE ROLE OF PLANNING IN TEACHER PREPARATION

Miranda, a college sophomore, has just completed her first attempt to plan and teach a lesson to a small group of preschoolers while enrolled in her first methods course, Education of Young Children. It is a basic psychological principle that human beings under stress revert to what is familiar; aspiring teachers are no exception. Like many early childhood majors who are assigned to teach their first lesson, Miranda relies on her memories as a young child. She fondly recalls carving a pumpkin and roasting the seeds back when she was in kindergarten, so this is where she begins. Miranda's experience with planning might have stopped there if the instructor, Dr. Conrad, had not been expecting more. First, Miranda is tying the activities she has planned to academic standards issued by the leading organization in her field, the National Association for the Education of Young Children. Second, through some creative scheduling, Miranda will be engaging in a discussion about the plan, not with her fellow sophomores, but with two juniors, Kaylee and Rachael. They completed the course previously and are well acquainted with the lesson review process; excerpts of their lesson-meeting discussion are in Figure 3.1. Finally, Miranda will be submitting a reflective journal entry that analyzes her experience of planning and teaching. These opportunities make interactive methods of lesson planning part of the repertoire of these future teachers.

PLANNING AND FIELD EXPERIENCES

The transition from the theoretical information obtained in a university classroom to the practical application of teaching can be difficult. In the university classroom, students have learned to formulate lesson plans but without the opportunity to really know their students and/or the curriculum of the school where they will complete their fieldwork. Davenport and Smetana (2004) identify field experiences as the most significant part of any teacher preparation program. It is during these field experiences that teacher candidates actually take responsibility for lesson planning, instructional implementation, and assessment of student learning. Student teachers need to see this design work as part of a teacher's work and as routine practice. Although valued by student teachers, field experiences, from a teacher education perspective, sometimes are seen as destroying what students have learned in their campus classes. University professors encourage preservice teachers to collaborate with others when planning; however, when they enter the field, beginning teachers may see experienced teachers working in isolation and be expected to do the

---

Figure 3.1 Preservice Teachers Discuss a Lesson Plan

Miranda is a sophomore who has written her first plan in a methods course. Kaylee and Rachael are juniors who completed the course previously and have read Miranda's lesson plan. Miranda describes how she presented a pumpkin activity lesson during the month of October to a preschool class. First she read a book called *The Runaway Pumpkin* by Kevin Lewis (2003) that introduced how pumpkins grow, where they come from, and how to carve them. She presented a song chart with "The Five Little Pumpkins." Finally she had the children work in small groups on file folder games with initial consonants.

RACHAEL: What would you say was the best part of the lesson that you definitely would do again if you were teaching the lesson?

MIRANDA: I loved the story and song. I love reading stories! I think it's so crucial to their education. I wanted an interactive way to get them involved and so I tied in the file folder game idea. Even though they had a little trouble with the letter associations—and just a few of them did—I would definitely say the file folder game. They were excited and anxious to start it. I think it was good, but certainly next time I would just explain it a little better.

RACHAEL: You said that you provided the words so that they would match the words with the letters?

MIRANDA: Right. Inside the file folders was a pumpkin with an initial consonant on it. There were various letters, probably five or six with each file folder. Then on the envelope on the back, I included stems to the pumpkins that had words beginning with the letter on them with Velcro. Children matched the words on the stems to the correct letter and pumpkin.

RACHAEL: Another option that you might consider is using pictures. Use pictures such as a cat for "c" and match it that way.

KAYLEE: Yes, to start them out, then later on when they have developed and are used to the words, they could go on.

RACHAEL: On the other hand, what is the part that you'd want to change? Something that you thought didn't go as well as it should have?

MIRANDA: Since it was my first time teaching in a preschool setting, I actually think it was the story. I think it was maybe too long. I had trouble toward the last third of the story keeping their attention. I continued to try to ask questions with each page. A couple of them would shout things and such, but I felt like I was sort of losing them the last third. So maybe choose a book that was shorter.

KAYLEE: Another thing that you could add to your lesson and you wouldn't even have to change your book is you could have them do actions throughout the story that would keep them involved.

MIRANDA: True.

KAYLEE: For example, every time they heard the word "pumpkin," or a certain word, they could do an action.

MIRANDA: That's a great idea!

KAYLEE: If you really liked the story you wouldn't have to change it then.

MIRANDA: Right.

RACHAEL: As you were reading the story, what types of questions did you ask?

MIRANDA: To start the book, I explained pumpkins. I had a little paper that I kept to myself. We discussed how pumpkins grow and what season we usually see them in. I asked, "Has anyone ever carved a pumpkin at home?" and, "Has anyone ever visited a pumpkin patch?" The previous week the class took a field trip to a pumpkin patch so they really had a lot to say about it. Throughout the story, I asked predicting questions such as, "What do you think will happen next?" There is a family in the story, so I'd ask, "What family member do you think we'll see next?" to keep them involved. I think they liked it... I sure hope so.

RACHAEL: Predicting definitely does help.

MIRANDA: Yes, that's what I've found to work.

RACHAEL: This is the first time you've used the academic standards, right? What did you think about that?

MIRANDA: Actually, as I was searching through the packet to determine which standards I felt were appropriate, I really enjoyed it and read through even the ones that didn't apply. I think they're the basis for a lot of things in education. It was interesting to see, on that level—a preschool level—what would be expected. All in all, I would say the children definitely achieved the standards and responded well. I enjoyed sticking to the standards.

KAYLEE: Did they help guide the lesson?

MIRANDA: Yes, they did. I found that one lesson could cover so many standards. I probably could've listed more.

RACHAEL: You get used to reading through page upon page [of standards]! For closure to the story, you might complete an activity like using the song again with finger puppets and having them do the motions with you.

MIRANDA: Right.

KAYLEE: I know you said in your reflection paper some children were doing the motions. You could teach the motions first and make sure each student is doing them.

MIRANDA: That was certainly something I sort of struggled with. That's something you sort of go with while you're there. I felt that as I introduced, I talked about everything relating to pumpkins, but then toward the end I just wasn't sure how to close it. That would be a good idea.

KAYLEE: Even when I write lessons and someone else reads over them, they think of tons of ideas. And it's not that any of your ideas are wrong. You could bring in pumpkin seeds for the children to taste and a pumpkin for them to see. Something that they can touch, that could be a manipulative.

RACHAEL: Every time you write a lesson, you need to think, "What will the children be doing?" Every activity we do, "What will their behavior be like?" And think, "If I were a 4-year-old, what would I be doing while waiting?" It's definitely something good to remember as you write more lessons. Always have something for them to do.

MIRANDA: Right.

RACHAEL: Always expect behavior problems and then know you can stop them. Prepare for the worst.

MIRANDA: Right.

KAYLEE: You said that some children had a problem understanding what you wanted.

MIRANDA: Right.

KAYLEE: A good idea too would be to have them repeat what they think they're supposed to do. And that way you'd understand what they were having problems understanding.

MIRANDA: True. Their primary teacher . . . that was one thing I was very impressed with. She was constantly reiterating the rules. She'd call on some students and ask, "When we line up, what do we do?" That was a great technique that I found.

RACHAEL: It helps a lot to observe someone else too.

MIRANDA: Certainly.

KAYLEE: For assessment, your objectives and assessment—if you have four objectives, you should end up with four assessments.

MIRANDA: Okay.

KAYLEE: So assessment for each objective—you said something about listening in your objectives—listening to the demonstration of roles.

MIRANDA: Right.

KAYLEE: So you'll need to assess that.

RACHAEL: Your special needs adaptations were good. Did you have any students with special needs in your class?

MIRANDA: I actually didn't. The only concern that the teacher mentioned is that she did have a lot of students at very different academic levels. So that was something I grappled with and it sort of came out in the lesson also. I tried my hardest to keep them on the right track. Like I said in my lesson, I stood in close proximity to the students. I was right there at their tables and I spoke loudly and clearly. I monitored their progress as they were continuing through the file folder game and of course assisted when needed. All in all that was the only concern.

KAYLEE: About how many children did you teach?

MIRANDA: There were 18 children.

RACHAEL: And they were all 4-year-olds?

MIRANDA: Yes, just 4-year-olds.

RACHAEL: Sometimes, as you mentioned, adapting to different ability levels is challenging. It is important to make sure you cover all of their needs.

MIRANDA: I was fortunate. The teacher allowed me several times to do a checklist of where the students are academically. It was interesting to see their different levels also. I tested them on colors and their addresses, but you can see the difference in their levels certainly.

KAYLEE: It's good that you were able to use a checklist too.

RACHAEL: I think checklists can be beneficial. I like them. One thing that we talked about (in class) with checklists is that you need to use the information. Once you actually check everything off, make sure you use the information that you found. Make sure you apply the information. It can be very beneficial. Your materials were good. You covered all of the things you needed.

KAYLEE: You did a nice job!

MIRANDA: Thank you. I was nervous doing my first one [lesson]. Thank you!

same. The teaching of planning to preservice teachers and the reteaching of planning to veteran teachers needs to be consistent. The practice of planning is just as important as the practice of teaching. It has to be treated as a simulated practice with reflective backtalk as part of the planning, so that the student teachers have the experience of naming and framing as well as reframing, and become used to formulating and discussing the meaning of information. In order to develop into competent professionals, student teachers need experience in the practice of reflective curriculum planning (Carlgren, 1999).

When preservice teachers are planning, it is imperative that they know their students. Freiberg (2002) wrote that teachers make instructional decisions on the basis of the learner (Who are my students?), content (What information, ideas, and concepts do I want my students to grasp?), and context (Under what conditions will instruction occur?). Dorph (1997) asked the following questions:

- How do teachers learn to consider content from the standpoint of their students?
- How do they make a shift from thinking about what they know and care about to what students need to learn and what students are likely to find interesting, puzzling, or significant?
- How do they learn to frame questions that invite multiple possibilities rather than one right answer?
- How do they build discussion around the students' ideas?
- How do they develop the habits and skills to monitor their practice and its impact on students?

These questions extend the agenda for teaching from considerations of subjects to considerations of pedagogy. The focus shifts from what teachers know and believe about their subjects to learning opportunities for students: how teachers design, adapt, and implement lesson plans, and how they work with colleagues to improve their teaching.

Since these are central tasks for teachers, it makes sense to work on them with preservice teachers in the context of teaching through on-site assistance and support during fieldwork (Dorph, 1997).

A college junior arrived at his field placement site, a public school program for 4-year-olds, 15 minutes after the children had been assigned to their small groups with each preservice teacher. The practicum student had been warned about being late on two previous occasions when he arrived after the other college students had already begun their lessons. Lack of planning was evident when he did not have the appropriate materials needed for the children, forgot the questions he was going to ask, and inadvertently omitted the closure of the lesson. When the college faculty member responsible for supervising the student took him aside and made it clear that this was unacceptable, the student responded angrily, "You're treating us like teachers!" Just 1 year separated this young man from student teaching, just 2 from full responsibility for an entire class of children.

This situation captures a universal dilemma confronted by teacher educators as they are surrounded by those human, professional "works in progress" called preservice teachers. More often than not teacher educators' recommendations are predicated on promise and potential rather than polished performance. Collaborative planning is one way to build prospective teachers' confidence and skills and, in so doing, to build greater trust in our teacher candidates' abilities. Suppose that, instead of assigning students to write the reams of lessons, units, themes, and projects that weigh down briefcases and tote bags each semester, teacher educators focused on quality instead of quantity. Professors would engage prospective teachers in planning that takes a page from the Japanese lesson meeting by addressing actual classroom lessons that are observed by others, planning over a longer period of time, focusing on relevant academic standards and appropriate educational goals, and recording, discussing, and revising plans with an eye toward improvement (Lewis, 2000). Collaborative planning and lesson study immerses preservice teachers in "a continuous cycle of classroom problem solving—a Plan, Do, Check, Act process"—and "holds the promise of fundamentally redesigning the process of teaching" (Wilms, 2003, pp. 606–607).

Research by McCutcheon (1980) serves as a reminder that teacher planning is a complex process involving both written plans and mental planning. Planning is enhanced when teachers' writing and thinking are joined through the problem-solving mode of reflective thought suggested by Dewey (1910). This reflective thought can be stimulated through probing questions (Weeks, 2001). These probing questions could be posed and discussed during class or in individual consultation with students, or stimulated through the review of curricular materials such as state academic standards, district curriculum guides, or lesson plans posted online (Newfield, 1982). In the current educational climate it is surprisingly easy for teacher educators to forget that the goal is not to stuff undergraduates' heads with content knowledge and the rudiments of pedagogy. If we do succumb to that pressure, we can be certain that at least some students will memorize (and quickly forget) material for the test and take the safe path of proposing routine lessons. Preservice teacher education would be better served if teacher preparation programs aimed higher, at the development of wisdom, during the planning process. Sternberg (2004) proposes ways to teach wisdom, which we apply here to preservice and novice teachers.

- Provide novices with real and relevant issues of practice that demand wise thinking, such as incorporating the multiple intelligences into lessons that are aimed at preparing students for high-stakes, standardized tests.
- Maintain a focus on the common good—an emphasis on balancing the interests of all stakeholders—throughout the planning process. This involves knowing students, understanding learning styles and interests, and knowing the school curriculum.
- Provide past examples of teachers' wisdom of practice and analyze them; role-model wise teachers' thinking for students without making solutions appear facile. This could be accomplished through watching a DVD or videotape of a teacher who needs to make multiple decisions throughout a lesson.
- Promote dialectical thinking in preservice teachers to illustrate that responses to problems in teaching are seldom simple or neatly categorized as right or wrong. More often definitions of better and worse solutions vary according to sociocultural context. This can be accomplished through a strong focus on multicultural education.
- Show students in teacher preparation programs that their instructors, mentors, and supervisors value wise information processing and wise solutions. Everyone involved with the students needs to give these preservice teachers opportunities to research, problem-solve, and make decisions. Have them debate the solutions and decisions, and devise a plan for best practices.

Through reflection and collaboration during field experiences, preservice teachers will learn to diminish ineffective or moderately effective lessons and create rich, engaging lessons for students. As one student teacher said, "Not every teacher comes up with the best ideas on his or her own." Teachers need not be experts in every subject or on every topic, when they can capitalize on the knowledge and instructional approaches of colleagues. Writing objectives collaboratively to meet state and national standards, incorporating higher levels of thinking and learning, utilizing motivational techniques to "grab" the students' attention, and using logical and sequential hands-on activities to facilitate student learning of the objectives are vital pieces of an effective lesson. Asking questions that prompt students to think critically and analyze information is not always easy but can be accomplished if two or three educators work together to develop those questions. Another challenge of good teaching is not only assessing or evaluating the work of students but also teaching them to self-assess their work. It is often necessary to tap the minds of colleagues to be certain that all students are meeting the standards and becoming critical thinkers and information processors.

COLLABORATIVE PLANNING FOR PRESERVICE TEACHERS

Mary and Greg were student teachers in the same building, Greg in kindergarten and Mary in second grade. The two were nervous yet eager to begin their preservice experience. Greg was having some problems with discipline in the early stages of his teaching, and Mary was struggling with formulating questions appropriate for her second graders. Both student teachers were challenged by time management; Mary's lessons tended to last too long, whereas Greg's ended too quickly. Also, based on supervisory comments, both preservice teachers had concerns about word usage and functioning as language role models for their students.

Many student teachers experience such difficulties, but what makes these two preservice teachers different is that they chose to collaborate to improve their planning and teaching. Along with getting feedback from their cooperating teachers and university supervisors, this pair of preservice teachers worked with each other as part of a collaborative project. The two met on a weekly basis and supported each other through the experience even though it required an extra time commitment. In the spring and fall semesters of 2004, these two student teachers, and three student teachers in another building, volunteered to participate in a Peer Collaboration Project. These enthusiastic preservice teachers were told about the concept of Japanese lesson meetings and how American educators were looking for ways to adapt the Japanese model to be used in U.S. classrooms.

The students met with one of the project coordinators—a teacher educator with 17 years of experience as a teacher and 2 years as a building administrator—to learn the details of conducting such a collaborative meeting. The preservice teachers were informed that the purpose of the assignment was to use their colleagues as resource people who could help contribute to their professional development. They were to identify either lessons that were less than satisfactory or other problems such as classroom management, lesson timing, student discipline, lesson motivation, and so on. Next they were to solicit ideas from their peers and consult professional literature that could help them to improve in these areas, and then utilize those ideas and findings in the classroom. Study group members were given a few ground rules, such as listening carefully to one another, asking questions for clarification, and providing positive feedback, concrete suggestions, and constructive criticism based on theoretical knowledge, observations of other teachers, and past experiences. They were to arrange observations of one another, meet in advance to focus their observations, and confer afterwards to provide timely and constructive feedback.

The student teachers were given a sample agenda to follow in their collaborative meetings. The first few minutes were to be allotted to the teacher who was sharing the problem. The next few minutes were to be used for the other members of the group to ask clarifying questions. When using a lesson plan, the members were to read and analyze the plan and accompanying student work, if provided. Next, the group was to provide feedback, both positive and critical. The final minutes of the meeting were to be used for reflection, debriefing, and open discussion. The students were told that they could invite the project coordinator to attend a session; however, that was not a necessary component. Finally, the student teachers were asked to write an overall reflection of the Peer Collaboration Project. The following is a vignette that was produced by Mary and Greg, the two student teachers introduced earlier.

In the beginning, Mary and Greg discussed the units and daily plans that they were using in their classrooms and shared ideas for motivation techniques, hands-on activities, and discipline strategies that would enhance various lessons. As the semester progressed, they observed each other in the classroom, reflected on strengths and areas needing improvement, and made changes in their methods of planning and delivering instruction. For example, Greg had difficulty getting students to understand subtraction. He claimed that after the first day of instruction, even though the lesson seemed to go well, many students still did not understand the concept. Mary suggested that Greg start again and use the base-10 blocks so that the students could visualize the process. After Greg implemented this suggestion, the students' performance improved.

Similarly, after Greg observed Mary's reading lesson, he complimented her on her use of higher-level questioning skills. He noticed, however, that the students were not being attentive during the oral reading of the story, so one suggestion he had was that she use more voice inflection when reading to young children to capture their attention and encourage them to listen attentively. He also noticed that the children were noisy as they returned to their seats after the story and that because they were talking, it took them quite a bit of time to get back on task. A strategy that he used with his children was to count to 3, and all students were to go quietly back to their seats, then look at him to begin their next activity. Mary acted on Greg's suggestions and was pleased with the results.

At the end of their student teaching semester, Mary and Greg commented on the value of collaboration. Both had passed their student teaching, and they attributed their success partially to their collaborative efforts. They also vowed to continue collaborating with colleagues. Although some might argue that preservice teachers collaborating is a case of "the blind leading the blind," Mary and Greg had different strengths, built mutual trust and respect, and saw evidence that working together had helped them to improve their teaching.

Encouraging Reflection

Reflective practice is widely acknowledged as a marker of growing expertise, yet it is not uncommon for preservice teachers to ask, "What am I supposed to reflect on?" or, "What do I do with all of this reflection?" Even well-established reflective practitioners can be so immersed in a fast-paced, test-score-driven school culture that those skills can atrophy from disuse or disregard by others. Irrespective of experiential level, some teachers wait to be told exactly what to do or persist in a futile quest for the one, best method that works with every child. It is possible for educators at all levels of experience and positions in the educational field, from preschool through graduate school, to remain at a "received knowing" stage (Belenky, Clinchy, Goldberger, & Tarule, 1997). Here the assumption is that every question has a definitive answer that someone else knows.

Typical of this approach was a question that dominated the conversation between a college professor and a group of student teachers in a weekly seminar. They would meet on campus one afternoon a week, and most of the student teachers' questions would begin with, "What do you do with a child who . . . ?" Their professor usually asked for more information, then began her reply with the phrase, "It depends." One student said, with a tone of exasperation in her voice, "You always say that!" The professor agreed that she did use that phrase often, an admission that the class found amusing. "But here's a question for you: Why? Why does it depend? If a friend tells you, 'Guess what, I'm getting married. Do you think it's a good idea?' how would you respond?" For this group of young adults, that question seemed to hit home; the answer truly was, "It depends." The issue of responding to a child's behavior is just too complicated and important for a one-sentence answer. Teachers must reflect on the situation and develop several answers from which to choose, understanding that there is more than one defensible approach or course of action.

Disillusionment often sets in as preservice teachers begin with a large measure of idealism that runs up against the harsh realities of the world of work. Preservice teachers often fail to recognize the idealism and romanticism that they have about children and teaching. The hopeful dream that simple solutions exist to all of a teacher's challenges is at odds with much of the theory and research on teachers' professional development as well as the realities of classroom practice (Schon, 1983, 1987). When working with children, there are no "simple solutions"; rather there are often multiple solutions that are very complex. Educators must learn to investigate all possible solutions and make decisions that benefit the learners.

Autumn, Erin, and Rebecca completed their student teaching in a building different from Mary and Greg. The three student teachers also worked on the Peer Collaboration Project with the same university supervisor as Mary and Greg. Their comments regarding the benefits of collaboration follow:

> "During our meetings, we each discussed things that we would like to improve upon. It was refreshing to hear the ideas that were suggested by my peers. Throughout our meetings we were also able to give one another lesson ideas. In my particular student teaching experience, I was having problems with classroom management, and they both [Autmn and Rebecca] gave me great ideas on different strategies and techniques to implement." (Erin)

> "I know I was having major difficulties teaching the 20-minute portion of the math lessons and for the life of me I couldn't get the lessons even close to the allotted time frame. I talked to other student teachers, and they helped me to develop ideas that would help reduce the time I was using to teach the portion of the lesson that was to be completed within 20 minutes. It helped greatly. I still didn't meet the time requirement but I was close, cutting the lesson from about 40 minutes to 25 minutes. This made a huge difference so I was very thankful for their thoughts on the topic." (Autumn)

> "In our many meetings, my peers provided me with a variety of helpful strategies that enabled me to improve my classroom management and teaching techniques. One of the areas that I felt I needed to improve upon the most was classroom management. Through conversing with the other student teachers, I was able to greatly improve in this area. The teachers suggested a variety

of classroom management techniques, like using more intrinsic motivational comments, individual behavior guideline charts, and nondisruptive cues for appropriate and/or inappropriate behaviors. All of the suggestions from my peers were helpful and useful to me." (Rebecca)

As discussed by these and the previous student teachers, preventing academic failure and behavior problems from occurring in classrooms, supporting students' academic progress and appropriate behaviors, and correcting discipline problems when they do occur are some of the biggest challenges faced by teachers today. Classroom management problems are also a leading reason for preservice teachers' dissatisfaction with their ability to fulfill the professional role of teacher. Time management, lesson momentum and smoothness, and creating a positive learning environment are all important aspects of classroom management. By learning effective management strategies, through observation and collaboration, new teachers can eliminate many problems before they become major concerns.

Over the next several years, the nation will need to fill over 2 million teaching positions (Peter Harris Research Group, 2004). Darling-Hammond (1997) stated that most U.S. teachers begin their careers in disadvantaged schools where turnover is highest. These new teachers are assigned the most educationally needy students. They are given the most demanding schedules with many extra duties, and receive few resources and no mentoring. She said that after such "hazing," many choose to leave the profession and others merely learn to cope rather than to teach well. Among the many "needs to know" for teachers, Darling-Hammond contends that teachers need to know about collaboration. They need to understand how to collaborate with other teachers to plan, assess, and improve school-wide learning. Teachers need to be able to reflect on and analyze their own practice in order to assess the effects of their teaching and refine and improve their instruction. Teachers learn as their students do—by studying, doing, and reflecting; by collaborating; by looking closely at students and students' work; and by sharing what they see (Darling-Hammond, 1997, 2006).

Asking questions of their practice may be one of the most significant techniques student teachers can learn to make themselves into better educators. They need to learn to reflect on their strengths, what goes well with each lesson, and whether the students have met the lesson objectives, as well as what they can improve upon to make the best learning atmosphere for their students. Being a reflective practitioner means constantly evaluating personal effectiveness as an educator (Kauchak, Eggen, & Carter, 2002).

Recognizing the Value of Collaboration

Parkay and Stanford (2001) wrote that the heart of collaboration is meaningful, authentic relationships among professionals. Such relationships do not occur naturally; they require hard work and commitment. Collaboration has at least seven distinctive attributes. Collaboration is

- Voluntary so that teachers make personal choices to collaborate
- Based on parity to allow all individuals' contributions to be valued equally
- Focused on a shared goal
- Founded on shared responsibility for key decision making
- Designed to create shared accountability for outcomes
- Based on shared resources so that each teacher contributes something
- Emergent so that as teachers work together, shared decision making, trust, and respect increase

All of these characteristics were evident in the Peer Collaboration Project with the student teachers. The preservice teachers valued one another's input, mentioning that they learned important time management and classroom management skills from each other. They had a shared goal of improving their teaching and management techniques, shared their knowledge and resources, and built increasing trust and respect for one another. Several student teachers mentioned that they became more than just acquaintances; they also became responsible and trusted colleagues. One student teacher described the value of learning what was happening in other classrooms in other grade levels.

> In addition to gaining valuable classroom strategies, the meetings allowed the other student teachers and me to find out what was being done in the various grade levels. For instance, I was teaching third grade, and I thought it was extremely helpful to learn how second grade was preparing their students for the content that they will need for the third grade.

Through collaboration, teachers gain insight into what is happening in other classrooms at various grade levels. In many schools the primary wing does not know what the intermediate wing is doing. Teachers appreciate knowing what basics the students learned before reaching a particular grade level, and what students need to know and be able to do before advancing to the next grade level. Instead of wasting valuable instructional time trying to figure out the learning styles of their students, through collaboration they learn from other teachers what instructional strategies are helpful to individuals and groups of children. Thus, when writing curriculum, it is easy to scaffold it in a way that children will not be left behind in a subject area as a result of poor curriculum design. Also, through collaboration, teachers in different disciplines can see and hear what is going on in other classrooms and work toward a more integrated approach. When students make connections, learning becomes more valuable and meaningful. As one student explained:

> When the three of us met, it gave us a chance to get to know one another on a more personal level. Prior to student teaching, I knew Becky [Rebecca] and Autumn from classes; however, through this project, we all became good friends. During some of the stressful parts of the semester, it was nice to know that I could talk openly and honestly with them and get advice about different things that were happening. Furthermore, I was able to get to know the other student teachers on a personal level. Before these meetings, we would pass one another in the hallway with a polite "Hello"; however, now I feel we have grown a lot closer because we shared our experiences together. It was nice to know that there were others going through the same problems that I was.

Enjoying one's work and the people one works with is half the battle. By working in teams, teachers get to know one another not only on a professional basis, but on a personal level as well. This can develop into more of a family or community atmosphere that creates a more positive, caring learning culture within a school setting.

In a 1999 report from the U.S. Department of Education, two-thirds of beginning teachers reported no formal induction program during their first year of teaching, with only 19% of new teachers assigned to a mentor teacher. Many teachers are still expected to teach in isolation, which can make the profession more challenging and more frustrating than it has to be. Fullan and Hargreaves (1996) stated that teachers are not islands and they do not develop in isolation; rather, they develop through relationships. Isolation gives teachers a certain degree of discretion to exercise their own judgments; however, it also cuts teachers off from clear and meaningful feedback about the worth and effectiveness of what they do. Dorph (1997) agrees that feedback is particularly important for novices because teachers must find ways to make content important and meaningful to their students. They cannot simply tell students what they have figured out for themselves. Even when teachers work with prepared materials, they still have to determine what they want students to learn, decide what strategies are appropriate for teaching what they want students to learn based on individual students' learning styles, anticipate student responses, and adapt teaching suggestions to suit their own situation. To teach for comprehension, teachers must know more than facts, concepts, and so on. They must understand how ideas fit together and how new knowledge develops. Effective teachers anticipate what students are most likely to find difficult and give clear explanations, ask good questions, design authentic learning experiences, and assess student understanding (Dorph, 1997). Uncertainty, isolation, and individualism are a "potent" combination that undermines a sense of community in schools (Fullan & Hargreaves, 1996). Teaching is a lonely occupation for those who need adult companionship and adult interaction (Schlechty, 1990).

Preservice teachers need to find the tools necessary to create engaging learning experiences for their students. Elementary teachers, especially, typically teach three to five subjects a day, and it can be difficult to develop hands-on, creative lessons for each subject. Jackson (2004) suggested that changes occur in student teachers as they transition from their first days of student teaching to becoming experienced professionals. She stated that these changes involve the need for affirmation and professional nurturing. Student teachers eventually begin to encourage one another with appropriate comments and suggestions for improvement. Differentiating instruction for students is a complex challenge that can be met effectively when teachers meet and plan together, spend time in one another's classrooms, share lessons and materials, and take turns watching and coaching one another (Tomlinson, 1999). Collaboration offers teachers the opportunity to share ideas, to get to know one another, and to develop mutual trust in and respect for teaching colleagues (Johnson, 2006).

MEETING THE NEEDS OF NOVICE TEACHERS
THROUGH COLLABORATIVE PLANNING

Overall I liked the idea of working with peers to help one another in the teaching profession. I felt that being able to talk to another teacher and relieve stress on an issue was a great way to find a solution to whatever problem you may be seeking to correct. Becky, Erin, and I worked together on this project, and I think we all found it very helpful since we were all new to the daily routines of a full-time teacher. The meetings were short and to the point.

Many people refer to the first few years of teaching as the survival stage (Isenberg & Jalongo, 1997). This is the stage where teachers do what they can to keep children occupied and out of trouble in the classroom, try to keep up with the paperwork, meet with parents to build positive relationships, assume out-of-classroom duties, and so on. Collaboration can assist teachers in moving from the survival stage to having a real impact on young learners by helping new teachers realize that they are not alone with their problems.

Based on data trends reported by the National Center for Education Statistics, it is necessary but not sufficient just to attract excellent teachers to the profession. The greater challenge appears to be, first, preparing a teaching force that represents the diversity in the United States and, second, retaining teachers once they are employed. Induction/mentoring programs are now a requirement in most states to help with the retention of new teachers. Principals and other administrators grapple with ways to provide help and support for those just entering the brave new world of teaching. Many are looking at new and improved collaboration models to support beginning teachers, enhance the knowledge and skills of veteran teachers, and ultimately benefit students so that they can develop and learn to their full potential.

Supporting New Teachers: The View from the Principal's Office (Peter Harris Research Group, 2004) took a comprehensive look at the involvement of the nation's school administrators in the recruitment, hiring, and retention of teachers. Their report is based on data collected from more than 600 in-depth interviews with public school principals throughout the United States. The specified sample groups were low-income/central-city schools, low-income/rural schools, and a national cross-section of all schools. These principals included those serving elementary, middle, and high schools.

Eighty-five percent of the principals in the study said that work-related stress is a serious issue for first-year teachers. Carlgren (1999) identifies a major source of that stress when she writes that it is impossible to "erase" in the classroom. The work of the practitioner is constrained by what has been called "the practical imperative." It is not possible for someone to try out an idea, and later change her mind. The right thing must be done at the right moment. And what is done cannot be undone. The administrators in the survey recommended that the stress could be relieved if teacher preparation focused more attention on real-world disciplinary problems and on the teaching demands of today's classrooms, as well as on developing stronger mentoring programs in schools. Forty-four percent of the principals surveyed reported that new teachers face problems related to classroom management above all, and 42% said that instruction and pedagogy were the biggest problems faced by new teachers. Peter (1994) wrote that experienced teachers have well-developed classroom routines and procedures as well as professional knowledge, which includes information and images on how typical lessons will run. Beginning teachers lack this knowledge and the experience upon which to make informed judgments. Almost two-thirds of the principals believed that education schools should do more to emphasize what it takes to manage a classroom, particularly by giving new teachers more exposure to experienced teachers and by providing them with practical strategies. A nearly unanimous 98% of the principals responded that teacher mentor programs make it more likely that students will receive a quality education.

Other countries are realizing the importance of a collaborative mentoring process. Darling-Hammond (1997) discovered that in Japan and Taiwan, a year-long supervised internship, with a reduced teaching load that provides time for mentoring and additional study, is a requirement for all teachers. Under Japanese law, beginning teachers receive at least 20 days of inservice training during their first year of teaching and 60 days of professional development. Master teachers are given release from their classrooms to advise and counsel novice educators. Early experiences in Taiwan and Japan include new teachers watching other teachers, discussing problems of practice, presenting and critiquing demonstration lessons, and working with groups of colleagues imagining and acting out how students might respond to certain presentations of material. Collinson and Ono (2001) mention that school organization in Japan prevents professional isolation. New teachers are assigned to classrooms beside experienced colleagues at the same grade level, and teachers share a common workroom for planning. Because schools in some other countries, such as Italy, are structured for this type of collaboration, teachers share knowledge and refine practices throughout their entire careers.

Professional growth is a necessary component of any professional field in all countries. This is especially true in teaching, as accountability and responsibilities seemingly increase daily. Each teacher in a collaborative group brings a special knowledge to the table. Some educators have a strong background in technology, others in assessment, and yet others in new and best practices in literacy. When teachers collaborate, they learn from one another, grow, and raise one another (and their students) to levels that they never dreamed possible. Collaboration encourages teachers to see change not as a task to be completed, but as an unending process of continuous improvement (Hargreaves, 1994). It is an important charge for school leaders to nurture professional communities for new and veteran teachers. The issue of time, admittedly a factor in collaborative efforts, can be and should be dealt with effectively so that meeting with colleagues is not just an added responsibility but an anticipated part of every new teacher's workweek.

MODELS OF COLLABORATION FOR NOVICE TEACHERS

As the needs for, and benefits of, working together to plan collaboratively in education become apparent, more and more models of collaboration are being tried. Johnson and Kardos (2002) reported research results from the Project on the Next Generation of Teachers that was conducted at the Harvard Graduate School of Education. The project was a 5-year qualitative study of 50 new Massachusetts teachers. The project identified the importance of site-based, ongoing, rich teacher collaboration across experience levels for effective new teacher induction. The authors found that what new teachers wanted in their induction was experienced colleagues who would take their daily dilemmas seriously, watch them teach and provide feedback, help them develop instructional strategies, model skilled teaching, and share insights about students' work and lives. An underutilized resource in today's schools is the shared expertise of the teachers that can be activated through collaborative planning.

Even though formal lesson study as used in Japan is not widely used in the United States, there are other types of collaborative planning in place. A summary of six models follows.

Integrated Professional Cultures

Johnson and Kardos (2002) found that in some schools teachers were fortunate to begin their careers in what the authors termed "integrated professional cultures." These were subunits within schools that encouraged ongoing professional exchange across experience levels. There was sustained support and development for all teachers, not just isolated opportunities for novice and/or veteran teachers. Evidence showed that teachers working in these integrated professional cultures remained in their schools and in public education at comparatively higher rates than their counterparts in veteran-oriented, or novice-oriented, professional cultures. New teachers benefited from the practical experience of veteran teachers, while veteran teachers often appreciated the recent training of new teachers in integrating technology and interpreting data from standards-based assessments. Schools that geared their professional development to all teachers served their educators well, thus enabling them to serve their students well (Johnson, 2006).

Professional School Communities

Senge (2000) wrote that it is becoming clear that schools can be re-created, made vital, and renewed by taking a learning orientation. This means involving everyone in the system in expressing aspirations, building awareness, and developing their capabilities together. Arbuckle (2000) stated, "It is clear that creating vibrant, collaborative cultures in schools and school systems is a vital strategy for individual and school development" (p. 325). Successful teachers single out their professional community as their source of motivation, the reason they do not burn out in demanding situations, and the foundation of their adaptability to today's students.

Professional school communities are marked by the following attributes (McLaughlin, 1994):

- *Reflective dialogue*—open and reflective conversations about situations, challenges, subject matter, teaching practices, and so on.
- *Unity of purpose*—collective focus and commitment to optimize the learning of students and professionals alike.
- *Collaboration and norms of sharing*—viewing sharing ideas and approaches as valuable, not as stealing others' intellectual property.
- *Openness to improvement*—taking risks and trying new ideas.
- *Deprivatization of practice and critical review*—responsibilities that extend beyond the classroom; sharing, observing, and discussing one another's practice on a daily basis.
- *Trust, respect, and renewal of community*—safe places to examine practices, try new ideas, celebrate important events, and acknowledge mistakes.
- *Supportive and knowledgeable leadership*—leaders who create conditions that foster professional community, a culture of interaction, and reflective dialogue.

New teachers need to feel comfortable engaging in conversations with other professionals. Reflections on teaching and learning practices are vital in personal growth and professional development. Comfort levels will increase as teachers meet more frequently and have open and honest dialogue. Once in a while, it is imperative for new teachers to remind one another that they are there for the students and they need to refocus their attention on their responsibilities to students to provide them with a safe, appropriate, and rich learning environment. As discussed earlier, new teachers are always looking for novel ideas and creative approaches to teaching. Most teachers tend to be sharing and caring individuals, and realize that they are there for students, not for personal gain. Novice teachers often are fearful of taking risks, not because they do not want to do what is best for children, but because they are afraid of a poor evaluation if the lesson does not go as smoothly as planned. Or, even sadder, they are afraid of being criticized by colleagues for deviating from the status quo. Observing one another has the benefits of not only helping those observed but also generating new ideas to incorporate into the observers' repertoires. Teachers' unions often discourage observations because they may become "evaluations"; thus, it is necessary to carefully structure the observation and feedback for new teachers.

These attributes are imperative in the recruitment and retention of new teachers. New colleagues need to feel safe and supported in making decisions and trying new ideas, and to believe that their achievements are acknowledged and appreciated. Many teachers forget that as important, or more important than, acknowledging their weaknesses and areas for improvement, celebrations can keep them recharged, renewed, and returning to our schools.

Arbuckle (2000) explained how teachers feel invigorated, challenged, professionally engaged, and empowered just because they teach in an atmosphere that nurtures professional community. However, a professional community does not develop by itself. Without guiding ideas related to teaching and learning, there is no sense of direction or purpose. Without organizational arrangements that reduce isolation and connect people and information, changes cannot become part of the school system's life. And without powerful methods and tools, people cannot develop the new skills and capabilities necessary for deep learning.

Reflective Practice Groups in Teacher Induction

In this model, a consortium of five midwestern colleges collaborated with a suburban school district in a first-year teacher induction program. Along with assigning mentors and offering monthly skill sessions, reflective practice groups (RPGs) were created. Each group comprised a district administrator, two to three mentors with their protégés, and a college faculty member. RPGs included both elementary and secondary teachers because the organizers believed that teachers would gain a broader instructional perspective from listening to one another's challenges. The process attempted to accomplish two primary goals: unburden teachers from their unsettling dilemmas in a supportive environment with a focus on professional growth; and probe and reflect on the following professional practice issues suggested by Smith (2003):

1. What are my teaching practices?
2. What are the teaching theories that drive these practices?
3. How did I come to teach this way?
4. What are my options to better assist students?

Figure 3.2 shows the 10-step process for RPGs. The incidents that were discussed during the RPGs were categorized according to school-year months using the following codes: student behaviors, academic problems, student-to-student conflicts, parent/teacher relationships, student and teacher clashes, teacher roles and responsibilities, teacher/teacher conflicts, systemic problems/issues, student/family issues, and outside pressures for the teacher. Participants whose episodes were analyzed by the group felt a sense of relief and support. The data from the project pointed out the need for shared reflection as an accepted norm within the teaching profession. The data also demonstrated that RPGs provided structure for probing and reflecting on professional practice for new teachers, veteran teachers, administrators, and teacher educators. RPGs may be one way to increase teacher effectiveness and professional satisfaction (Cady, 1998).

Figure 3.2 A Summary Process for Reflective Practice Groups

1. Convene the small group.

2. Each participant takes 2–3 minutes to share a personal situation that occurred in school and that the individual did not quite know how to handle.

3. Group chooses one episode for in-depth discussion.

4. Episode, including objective facts as well as personal emotions, is retold by the original individual. Other participants ask for further details if needed.

5. Participants take 5 minutes to think about and write hypotheses for the rationality behind the action taken by the teller.

6. Participants share the hypotheses and these begin to suggest the teaching theory behind the episode.

7. Teller responds, beginning to uncover some of the internalized knowledge, practice, and self-awareness associated with this episode.

8. Group discusses how the teacher during this episode has effects on students—What has the student learned from this?

9. Group discusses how things could have been handled differently.

10. Group summarizes and debriefs.

Adapted from Cady, 1998

Interdisciplinary Teaming

Although the composition of an interdisciplinary team may vary from school to school, the team typically consists of three to five teachers who could be experienced or beginning teachers, representing various content areas, and one or more building specialists (learning support, speech therapist, etc.). In some instances, youngsters are included in the process. These teams come together to find ways to meet the needs of diverse students in a heterogeneous classroom. The success of teaming often depends on the team members' recognition that it takes time to come together, reconcile differences among members, and establish a standard pattern of interaction. Teams find it beneficial to (1) establish an agenda, (2) assign roles (timekeeper, note-taker), and (3) create a mechanism that is acceptable for resolving differences. It is recommended that the entire problem-solving meeting should take no longer than 25 to 30 minutes and include the steps listed in Figure 3.3.

The emergence of teacher collaboration is one way to address diverse learner needs and encourage school personnel, especially novice teachers, to acquire new skills. The generative effects of collaboration can benefit students as educators work as a team to eliminate ineffective classroom practices and address the differentiated needs of students (Gable & Manning, 1999). Inexperienced teachers could benefit immensely from the experience of working in these teams with veteran teachers who are used to working with diverse learners.

Peer Coaching

Coaching has been characterized as an observation and feedback cycle in an ongoing instructional situation. It is a collegial approach to integrating skills and strategies into a curriculum, a set of instructional goals, a time span, and a personal style. Together, the teacher and the "coach" examine the use of instructional strategies, evaluate the effectiveness of observed lessons, and plan for future experiences. It is a problem-solving endeavor between the teacher and the coach (Joyce & Showers, 1981). Through peer coaching, teachers grow professionally by observing one another's teaching and providing constructive feedback. The practice encourages teachers to learn together in a safe environment (Parkay & Stanford, 2001).

An example of a peer-coaching model is School Innovation Through Teacher Interaction (SITTI), which was developed in response to professional development needs (Pierce & Hunsaker, 1996). SITTI is a cyclical model that begins with a common vision, identifies needs of the faculty, estab-

---

Figure 3.3 The Interdisciplinary Problem-Solving
Meeting Applied to Lesson Planning

Step 1. Team leader begins by introducing nonteam members, recording names of participants, and explaining exact purpose of the meeting (to develop a plan).

Step 2. Team leader assigns roles and reviews responsibilities of each role as well as expectations for all participants. All participants are expected to be involved in the planning process.

Step 3. Team leader restates the procedures for developing a plan to effectively teach the lesson while addressing the needs of students.

Step 4. Team discusses subject matter that is to be taught, examines aspects of the lesson plan, and identifies students who may have difficulty with standard delivery of instruction.

Step 5. Team leader initiates discussion aimed at reaching consensus regarding pupil-specific accommodation priorities that need to be included in the lesson plan. Team focuses on difficulties that students might experience, and members share pertinent information to resolve uncertainties. Leader may pose questions to guide discussion and focus the plan.

Step 6. Team leader introduces brainstorming phase to generate a list of possible solutions that could be incorporated into the lesson plan.

Step 7. Team leader shifts discussion to team decision making about a plan of instructional accommodation.

Step 8. Team discusses procedures for implementing the plan and ways to evaluate its effect on student performance.

Step 9. Team establishes follow-up procedures to help ensure that the plan is carried out as agreed.

Step 10. Team leader conducts an evaluation to determine member satisfaction of both the process and outcome of problem-solving meeting, and determines whether adjustments to the plan are warranted.

Adapted from Gable & Manning, 1999

---

lishes experts among the faculty who will act on those needs, provides support for change and improvement through peer coaching, and monitors the achievement levels of the students as indicators of effectiveness of the program. Peer coaching is considered an integral part of the SITTI model. The steps in peer coaching are as follows: (1) training in observational and feedback skills, (2) building team effectiveness, (3) developing action plans for each team member, (4) establishing a peer-observation schedule, (5) providing formative feedback after each observation, and (6) evaluating personal performance against previously set goals. The teachers using this model found that peer coaching increased collegiality and enhanced each teacher's understanding of concepts and strategies.

Preservice and novice teachers would greatly appreciate the opportunity to have, and benefit from having, a coach. The preservice or new teacher and the coach could set goals, observe each other's classrooms, provide feedback, and help each other to attain professional goals.

Team Teaching

In some schools educators "team teach" in order to share the responsibilities of two or more classes. They divide the subject areas between them, maybe one preparing lessons in math, science, and health; and the other, in reading and language arts. The division of responsibility also may be made in performance levels of students—one teacher may teach the "higher-level" readers and "lower-level" math students; and the other, the opposite groups (Parkay & Stanford, 2001). Other arrangements consist of grade-level teams at the elementary level, and disciplinary teams at the secondary level. These teams often work together on curriculum, planning units of study, planning appropriate lessons for a diverse student population, and discussing everyday teaching and management issues at their levels or in their disciplines. Typically there is no real structure to the meetings of these teams. They meet on an as-needed basis to make decisions and solve problems.

Team teaching is one way that new or inexperienced teachers can get assistance from colleagues as they begin their teaching careers. This model could give new teachers the opportunity to teach the subjects in which they are most comfortable and knowledgeable, as they learn the other disciplines. Also, this model gives new teachers the opportunity to work together on planning lessons and units that meet the curriculum goals of the district.

Models of collaboration for new teachers are summarized in Figure 3.4.

RECOGNIZING THE BARRIERS TO
COLLABORATION FOR NOVICE TEACHERS

The benefits of collaboration are numerous for preservice teachers, novice teachers, veteran teachers, administrators, university faculty members, and, above all, the learners. The positive aspects of peer collaboration far outweigh the negative. However, as discussed in Chapter 2, there are some barriers to peer collaboration. Three barriers that are particularly related to preservice and novice teachers are lack of time, "group think," and power struggles.

Figure 3.4 Models of Collaboration for Novice Teachers

MODEL	FOCUS	EXAMPLE
Integrated Professional Cultures	How can new and veteran teachers work together to provide the best learning opportunities for our students?	Novice and veteran teachers meet to discuss the latest technology and how they could apply it in their classrooms.
Professional School Communities	How can we, as school employees, encourage and maintain an open and caring environment for our students and ourselves?	A team of school employees meet to plan Back-to-School night. They plan how to share important educational information with parents and students, and how to involve parents in the school community.
Reflective Practice Groups	What are my teaching practices? What theories drive these practices? How did I come to teach this way? How can I better assist students?	Administrators, teachers (preservice and novice), and university professors meet to discuss the theory of evolution and how to best teach this theory to students.
Interdisciplinary Teaming	How can we best meet the needs of diverse students in a heterogeneous classroom?	A few classroom teachers from various content areas, a specialist, and sometimes the student meet to determine how a child with limited English proficiency can best be taught in the regular classroom.
Peer Coaching	What can we learn, and how can we improve instruction, by observing each other teach and providing constructive feedback?	A novice teacher observes a veteran teacher to see how that teacher effectively manages a classroom. The veteran teacher observes the novice teacher and provides feedback on how to improve transitions between topics.
Team Teaching	How can we combine our efforts to provide the most valuable learning experiences for our students?	Two veteran teachers have expertise in science and mathematics. The new teacher on the team earned a reading concentration. These teachers team-teach so that the students can learn from each teacher's knowledge and experience. Also, the new teacher can learn more about the other disciplines.

Lack of Time

During the Peer Collaboration Project, the student teachers noticed that finding the time to collaborate was one of the difficulties of the project. They realized that novice, and even experienced, teachers all have to overcome the barrier of time.

"The only downside to the weekly teacher meetings was the issue of time. It was tremendously difficult to find a time that was convenient for all three of us to meet."

"The only con to this project was finding time to go and observe one another. We tried to schedule observations; however, all three of us were teaching at the same times. If full-time teachers were to participate in peer collaboration, I believe they would come across some difficulties of observing one another teach a lesson."

"Teacher collaboration has some great benefits but there wasn't much time to collaborate. As student teachers we had quite a few things to do, just like full-time teachers. Our schedules didn't allow us to collaborate very much. I think given more time the project could show great success, but with the time problem there are restraints."

Teachers already have more to do than is possible during a regular workday. Adding one more element to a busy day's schedule is difficult, if not impossible, for novice teachers in many schools. Administrators are already grappling with ways to keep class sizes lower without hiring more personnel. Thus, teachers have tight teaching loads, typically with one preparation period a day, which is to be used for planning, checking papers, making parent phone calls, attending IEP meetings, completing clerical work, setting up for the next lessons, and all of the other work that needs to be accomplished before the end of the day. Often team members do not have preparation periods at the same time, making it impossible to plan together during regular school hours. After-school commitments, such as coaching responsibilities, club sponsorship, or home responsibilities, also preclude teachers from collaborative planning.

Preservice teachers may have the advantage of attending a class or a seminar that provides time for shared dialogue and planning. Novice teachers, however, typically do not have that advantage. It is important for administrators to realize the value of collaborative planning for new teachers and to provide time for new teachers to plan with their colleagues. This can be done through careful scheduling, which will be addressed later in the chapter.

"Group Think"

Sometimes collaborative group members, especially young and inexperienced teachers, may get caught up in the process of "group think." This happens when one or two individuals have an idea but are afraid to speak up because it is not popular with the majority. Therefore, everyone goes along with the majority, even though that might not be what would be best for the children or the school. Teachers may feel a loss of autonomy by being pressured to conform within their teams (Johnson, 2003). For example, new teachers may want to try new and innovative ideas as they teach their lessons, whereas some of their colleagues may want to teach from the text or from their old, and often outdated, lesson plans. The new teachers may feel intimidated about participating in peer planning.

New teachers need to be encouraged, not discouraged, to try new ideas and implement creative teaching strategies in their classrooms. When teachers observe one another, new teachers can earn the respect of veteran educators by modeling effective lessons and by demonstrating students' achievement gains. Again, administrators play a very important role in supporting new teachers as they implement teaching strategies that help students to achieve to their fullest potential.

Power Struggles

Any time a group of people get together, there are bound to be personality clashes. Some collaborative group members may struggle to be the leader. Others may try to block the progress of the group or devalue a particular individual. Backstabbing and dissension may occur as a result of the process (Johnson, 2003). Beginning teachers must be careful not to get involved in these conflicts, as they want to be considered team players and want positive comments relayed to their administrators. Effective administrators provide opportunities for all teachers, new and veteran, to assume leadership roles. The administrators, as well as the teachers, also should be trained in conflict-resolution strategies so that when conflicts do occur, they are resolved in a professional and nonconfrontational manner.

SUGGESTIONS FOR IMPLEMENTING
A COLLABORATIVE PROJECT

Research has shown that collaborative planning is a valuable experience for student teachers and novice teachers within a school setting. To achieve the benefits of collaborative planning, however, a project has to be properly implemented. Just because a group of teachers collaborate, success is not guaranteed. Several steps are recommended for successful implementation of a peer collaboration project with new teachers.

1. *Invite participation.* If teachers and other staff members are forced to participate, they may see this effort as just another passing trend in the field of education. Teachers need to feel ownership of the process. Invite novice and experienced teachers from different grade levels and different disciplines to be group members.

2. *Keep groups relatively small in number.* A group of five or six members allows for all individuals to be heard at each session. Small numbers are more manageable as far as scheduling and time constraints.

3. *Have ground rules.* Make it clear that roles (such as that of group leader) will change with each meeting. Remind participants that each member gets an opportunity to speak at each meeting, and each member's thoughts and opinions should be embraced and valued.

4. *Set a calendar of meeting dates and times.* If faculty and staff members pencil these dates in early in the school year, they are more likely to avoid meeting conflicts.

5. *Devise an approximate time limit.* Divide the meetings into segments and set approximate limits for each segment.

6. *Create goals to be accomplished at each meeting.* Set a purpose based on the teachers' needs. Each teacher should be able to choose a topic for discussion.

7 *Encourage questions and reflection.* Give group members an opportunity to question the teacher whose topic is being addressed. Then, have the teacher reflect on those questions and give a verbal response.

8. *Develop a plan.* Allow all group members to give suggestions and ideas for improvement or development. Then devise a plan that is comfortable for the teacher who has the issue.

9. *Debrief.* Review the problem/issue and the plan for intervention.

10. *Implement the plan.* Have the teacher go back to his or her classroom and try the recommended ideas. Encourage peer observations during the implementation phase. Meet before the observation to guide it, then meet again soon after the observation to provide positive feedback and constructive criticism.

11. *Evaluate the plan.* Have the teacher explain what changes were made during the implementation phase, and whether or not this improved student learning and/or behavior.

12. *If necessary, revise the plan.* If the original plan was not success-
    ful, develop a new course of action for the teacher.

As mentioned previously in this chapter, building administrators have
a crucial role in supporting the collaborative efforts of new and veteran
teachers. First of all, it is necessary for them to believe in the process and
realize that it can have a positive impact on student learning, the climate
and culture of the school, and professional development of teachers. Second, since time is such a huge factor, it is necessary to provide time for
teachers to collaborate. Sharon Porterfield, principal in the Armstrong
Area School District, utilized a creative scheduling approach and built in
one half hour per week for her teachers to be able to meet together. This
half hour was in addition to the teachers' regular planning time. Sharon
had to revamp her entire master schedule, including the schedules of the
regular classroom teachers and all specialists who worked in her building.
She was careful to build this time in on Wednesdays and Thursdays, as
those were the least frequently missed days of school. With this new planning initiative, Sharon also incorporated a "buddy program" where sixth-
grade students went to kindergarten classes to help teach early literacy
skills. The students were under the supervision of the Title I teacher and
speech/language clinician, thus freeing the classroom teachers to meet.
For record-keeping purposes, Sharon used a form to help everyone remain focused, and provide feedback to her if she was unable to attend
the group meeting. The form included the targeted standard, benchmark,
and/or competency as identified from the result of state or local assessments; a description of the lesson plan, time frame, and strategy used as
the instructional solution; and the results—measurable impact of the solution. Sharon repeated a thought expressed by Charlotte Danielson (1996)
that although such collaborative projects require a considerable investment of time, professional educators will find the time. Sharon admitted
that it took her close to 30 hours of planning, revising, and implementing
to develop a schedule that worked for all teachers and specialists in her
building.

Administrators need to take an active role in the process, although
they should not necessarily attend all meetings because some teachers
(especially novice teachers) might be intimidated and hesitant to discuss
problems and concerns. Administrators need to function as facilitators by
providing resources (especially time) and encouragement, and speaking
with the teachers who are participating in peer collaboration about the
process and what they are learning. Written documentation and periodic
progress reports should be provided to the administration.

CONCLUSION:
COLLABORATION AS A SOLUTION FOR TEACHER RETENTION

"I believe that the pros outweighed the cons. If it were not for this project, I would not have had the chance to know my colleagues as well as I did. One of the definite pros was the exchanging of creative ideas. It's through collaboration with peers and other sources that teachers get great ideas."

"I found the weekly meetings between the other student teachers and myself to be a complete success. In our meetings, two other student teachers and I were able to discuss many important issues that affected our student teaching experience."

"I believe the final and most important outcome of the meetings was how we grew as professionals. Through our meetings, all of the student teachers demonstrated ethical behavior and confidentiality in interacting with one another. Therefore, I would suggest that all teachers try to find time to meet with other educators to better improve their teaching methods."

Because of the serious challenges that new preservice or inservice teachers face when entering a classroom, providing opportunities for collaboration just might be one key component of keeping those teachers in our classrooms. Collaborative planning is one way to design more creative and motivational lessons to increase student achievement, help new teachers learn techniques to effectively manage diverse groups of learners, and provide opportunities for all teachers, both novice and veteran, to continue to learn and grow as professionals. Added benefits are the personal friendships and community atmosphere that develop within the school. With the increased emphasis on standards, and the high accountability for teachers and schools, collaborative planning is one approach that is needed in order to acquire and retain talented educators who will help learners achieve their highest potential and attain higher academic standards.

CHAPTER 4

Lesson Planning as Professional Development: Collaboration Among Experienced Teachers

It is a regional inservice day, and 83 experienced elementary teachers representing various schools and districts fill the room. Although the statewide tests occur in grades 5, 8, and 11, the pressures of those high-stakes examinations have trickled all the way down into kindergarten. The presenters' overall goals for the inservice series of four sessions across a 6-month period are to familiarize teachers with the state standards, suggest teaching strategies that will enable them to meet multiple standards, and get them involved in grade-level planning groups. The fourth and final goal is for the participants in the inservice series to produce lessons that can serve as a resource for others across the schools and districts.

The sessions are well received but the final goal of compiling teachers' exemplary lessons falls flat. Some of the teachers contribute no plans because they did not have time to do them. The few teachers who do suggest a lesson fall back on something that they admittedly picked up at a previous inservice. One group, for example, suggests teaching the main idea of a story by using a work glove with the words *Who, What, When, Where,* and *Why* written on the fingers in permanent marker. The glove gimmick gains uncritical acceptance from the teachers, even though it results in story details rather than a succinct statement of the main idea. Disappointingly, across 83 classrooms, no more than a handful of the teaching strategies go beyond the routine, predictable, and widely known. After one lesson idea gets an enthusiastic response, the teacher remarks, "Now everyone is going to copy it, and my kids will say, 'We already did this *last* year.'"

THIS SITUATION RAISES many questions about the role of collaboration and planning in experienced teachers' lives, such as, What is the "history" of their planning? What were they taught about planning during their teacher preparation programs? How has their planning changed over the years? Have they made any efforts to collaborate within discipline/grade level or across disciplines/grade levels? Was that collaboration satisfying? Why or why not? And, perhaps most pertinent to the topic of this book, What would it take to make collaborative lesson planning "work" in their particular school culture?

The thesis of this chapter is that "planning meaningful experiences for students is a basic requirement for successful teaching" (Panasuk, Stone, & Todd, 2002, p. 808). From preschool through graduate school, the teacher's role is to design and deliver learning experiences that are appropriate, relevant, and instructive, as well as capable of engaging the students and deepening their understandings. Lesson design, planning, delivery, and review are essential to effective practice.

Insight into the difficulties of experienced teachers with the lesson design and planning process comes from large-scale observational studies conducted in South Africa. Taylor and Vinjenvold (1999) found that direct instruction and recitation predominated in classrooms.

- Lessons were generally characterized by a lack of structure.
- Few activities that promoted higher-order thinking skills, such as investigations, were evident.
- Real-world examples were used often, but at a very superficial level.
- Little group work or other interaction occurred between and among students.
- Students did very little reading and writing, and if they did, it was of a very rudimentary type.

In a subsequent observational study that sought to analyze and address the professional development needs of South African teachers, the researchers' initial observations were that, generally speaking:

> Teachers did not state the specific learning outcomes and tended to focus mainly on the materials themselves and the procedural issues for working with materials.
>
> In these cases the teachers did not explain why they were using the materials or how the activity/materials would be used to achieve the content, the learning outcomes or conceptual goals of the lesson. In many of these cases there was great learner activity and obvious enjoyment but in the end it was hard to determine what had been learnt. (Onwu & Mogari, 2004, p. 173)

Over the years, research focusing on experienced teachers in the United States has generated similar findings. In the absence of specific training, very few teachers establish linkages between objectives, the instructional activity, and the methods of evaluation (Panasuk, Stone, & Todd, 2002).

COLLABORATIVE PLANNING DENIED

Stated plainly, when lesson design and review is treated as extraneous to the real work of teaching, other tasks can be expected to take precedence. Even though the format of written lesson plans changes dramatically after student teachers graduate and enter the teaching force (e.g., from several pages to a bulleted list), lesson planning may stagnate at the levels attained during student teaching. Often, the stage of lesson design is taken for granted, and lesson review frequently is limited to self-evaluation or observations by supervisory personnel rather than a peer review process.

> The scene was an inservice day for teachers in Kentucky, and shortly before the meeting began, the presenter was approached by an energetic young teacher. "Is this going to be a sit and git?" the teacher asked, with a wry smile on her face. When the presenter looked puzzled, the teacher went on to explain, "Sit and git is what we call it down south when you just talk and we just sit and listen. That's what we usually do at these meetings."

As this teacher's comment implied, professional development demands more than polite listening. Teachers need to see new strategies modeled, implement them in classrooms, and analyze the results in the company of colleagues. The precepts of constructivism that are so much a part of discussions about children's learning apply equally to teachers, for practitioners must construct their own learning rather than be expected to simply absorb information. If the goal is to move lessons in the direction of deepening learners' understandings, this requires concomitant changes in how professional development for experienced teachers is conducted and evaluated.

When continuous improvement is the goal, lesson planning is a dynamic, recursive, and cyclical process. Its value cannot be assessed by quantitative means alone. Evidence in at least three categories—teacher work, learner work, and peer attestation—has to be collected and analyzed (Radford, 1998).

- *Teacher work* includes such things as lesson plans of units taught, activities, and classroom methods used; notes on teachers' reflections before, during, and after teaching; insights into successes and failures; and accounts of problem-solving processes.
- *Learner work* includes classroom organization regarding individual pupil activity and/or groupwork, individual and/or group level of participation and confidence shown during lessons, completion of learning tasks, evidence of adaptations to support learners at all levels, and indicators of student interest, motivation, and engagement.
- *Peer attestation* includes letters, comments, or notes of commendations from principals, other teachers, district officials, parents, or other key informants regarding teachers' classroom performance. (Onwu & Mogari, 2004)

The case below illustrates what happens when a very different set of assumptions pertain. Here the expectation is that increases in the state-mandated assessments are the only type of evidence that matters and that teachers observe one another, not for the purpose of lesson planning, but for the purpose of enforcing compliance with traditional, linear lesson plans and reporting back to management.

CASE STUDY: "WE HAVE BEEN MEETING FOR 2 YEARS NOW . . . WHEN ARE WE GOING TO ACTUALLY DO SOMETHING?"

LARRY TINNERMAN

The focus of this case is a charter school that serves a population of over 300 kindergarten through eighth-grade students and is staffed by 26 teachers and 34 instructional aides. Ninety-nine percent of the children are eligible for free or reduced-price lunches, 74% of the school population is African American, and 42% of the students require special education services. In terms of the performance data that are public information, in 2004 only 6% of the 5th graders and 17% of the 8th graders met or exceeded standards in mathematics. Results in reading are slightly better, with 9% of the 5th graders and 21% of the 8th graders at or above the state standards in reading. In the 6 years of its existence, the charter school has had five different principals. The constant change in management styles has left much of the staff disillusioned about hoped-for initiatives and skeptical about promised changes. Recently, the board of directors mandated a drastic change in management style. The administration announced that it was going to institute a "collaborative" approach.

Primary issues identified as critical by staff and administration were:

1. Poor student performance on state tests
2. Frequent changes in management style
3. Behavioral management issues with students
4. Absence of curriculum integration across the various grade levels
5. High percentage of students requiring special education services

Clearly, the issues confronted by this organization are both serious and complex and are not restricted to planning alone. However, as one teacher noted, the administration continued to send out conflicting messages concerning lesson planning and curriculum at the school.

I find myself gravitating somewhat to the middle of the lesson plan continuum; in other words, in favor of flexibility yet seeking a clear expectation as to the direction of the lesson. As I have tried to move away from the traditional lesson planning process, I have met with increased resistance from the administration. I seek the flexibility (bad word with our administration . . . they interpret that to mean unstructured) to make each lesson relevant and take advantage of "teachable moments." Yet, every time teachers venture away from a prescriptive lesson plan, administrators respond with, "What about the standards?" "The content, the content!" The ability of the teacher to respond is constrained, and the students become restless and unruly. From my perspective, freeing up the lesson plan can make even a class disruption a method of teaching social skills to my students; it can become a topic of writing where students are given the ability to vent their frustrations, or a reading about the feelings that young adolescents have regarding authority, or a discussion on topics that are relevant at the moment to the student. Such flexibility is assessed by management as a failure to adhere to the preconceived lesson plan, even though that plan's objectives included writing an opinion paper, reading a story from one of the *Chicken Soup* series books, and developing team-building skills for class discourse and discussion. A colleague's remark summed up the situation at our school very well: "We have been meeting for 2 years now. . . . when are we going to actually do something?"

The administration formed several committees and charged each with addressing the issues identified by the staff. Most pertinent to the topic of this book was the work of the Curriculum and Instruction Committee. This group was responsible for examining current curricular practices, promoting cooperative learning among the teaching staff, and establishing a mentoring program for new faculty that was executed and overseen by other teaching staff members. The first charge of the committee was to have teachers visit and observe on an informal basis in one another's classrooms. The observations were scheduled, and the following criteria were established for the first round of observations:

1. Were the lesson plans available and complete?
2. Was the plan followed during the lesson?
3. What percentage of time were the students observed as being "on task"?

Attempts to implement these changes encountered the following roadblocks:

1. Many tenured teachers were very protective of their "turf" and very sensitive about having people enter their classroom. They were defensive about how they currently did things and resented recommendations for improvements. Apparently, some of the teachers had entered into a state of denial as to how poorly these students were being educated, because they were totally amazed by the students' low scores on the tests.
2. Overall, the teachers lacked a certain level of confidence in the institution's ability to effect real change. There were many meetings, many plans, and many potential solutions put forth with each change in the administration. The staff enthusiastically embraced these new ideas and set out to implement them. Unfortunately, in most cases, the administration was inconsistent in the support necessary to ensure success in the process, and solutions were abandoned almost before they were begun.
3. Insistence on the use of traditional lesson plans has stifled even the most enthusiastic members of the teaching staff. All lessons must be tied directly to the standards or the test anchors. All school activities have been curtailed until the state test scores improve appreciably. Every activity must be tied to a standard, or it is not accepted as appropriate. The focus on test scores has led to lessons that are stagnant, uninspiring, and content-

driven. Students grow increasingly restless with the constant worksheets and practice exams that keep reiterating the message that they are not "good at" schoolwork and are powerless to improve their performance.

4. The survival mentality of the administration to find a solution caused one reactionary decision after another to be made. Staff members were confronted with the need to have students do well on the statewide tests, yet many of the students were more than 2 years behind grade level in reading and math abilities. It is more than unreasonable to expect staff to increase students' achievement by more than 3 grade levels in less than 1 year.

Our analysis of this situation is that teachers need to cooperate and make important curricular decisions that affect their classrooms. Staff members, when they try new methods and cooperate to achieve important learning goals for students, need support, both from colleagues and the administration. The focus of staff observations should not be to "check up" on colleagues but to model, critique, and co-teach various lessons. The staff must be full and equal partners in the educational process. The purpose of peer observation is not to monitor a colleague's adherence to traditional lesson plans, but to develop more process-oriented, multilayered lesson plans that incorporate a wide range of skills. A multilayered plan can meet many students' needs, foster higher levels of engagement, and promote a positive learning environment. The groups are flexible, and students can move between and among the activities. An example of a layered lesson plan follows:

In a 7th-grade language arts classroom, student abilities range from proficient in writing to very rudimentary in ability. The plan (which is linked to the standards but flexibly so) calls for the students to write three paragraphs on their impression of the recent Illinois attempt to ban violent video games for teens.

- *Group A—Rudimentary writers.* This group will develop a set of questions to be asked of students in conducting an opinion poll of the topics at hand. This group will make use of tape recorders to help take down the responses of the interviewees. They also will add their own opinions to the tape. The questions will be limited to three.
- *Group B—Basic writers.* This group will take notes from various sources, including Group A and the prepared tapes, and create a rough draft that will be reviewed by Group C.

- *Group C—Proficient writers.* This group will prepare the final product, including the proofing and correction of previous members' efforts.

  In the end, members of all three groups will participate in the presentation of the final product to the class.

This planning method addresses the standards, yet allows each student to contribute at his or her own level in a meaningful way. Also, because the groups are flexible, students can move between and among them and "sit in" on any group that piques their interest.

Bear in mind that the primary purpose of charter schools was and is to have the freedom to explore nontraditional methods of education with nontraditional student populations. If a professional staff neglects to do this with lesson design, instructional strategies, and the overall curriculum, then they have failed to meet the mission of their particular school as well as the mission of the charter school movement in general.

PROFESSIONAL DEVELOPMENT
THROUGH LESSON DESIGN AND REVIEW

A new superintendent attends the inservice program planned for the district. It begins with a "motivational speaker" in the morning, followed by various workshops in the afternoon. The superintendent is surprised to see how truculent some of the teachers have become. Several are checking their e-mails on PDAs, talking, or reading the newspaper with a flourish. Afterwards, she conducts an anonymous survey of her staff and discovers that they are nearly unanimous in their criticism of the current approach to these professional development days, and most indicate that they want to focus on improving classroom teaching. In response, the superintendent proposes a very different approach. The staff agrees to participate in a series of four professional development days designed specifically for all middle school teachers in the district. The sessions will be presented by a principal, will focus on lesson planning, and will take an interactive approach.

On the first day, the principal leading the session announces that, as part of the training, names of participants will be selected at random to teach a lesson that meets the state academic standards. At the conclusion of the first day, a fourth-grade teacher groans as a slip with his name is drawn from a jar. He will be responsible for presenting a lesson to 52 of his peers when the group convenes again the next month. The teacher confides to a friend that he is nervous about the lesson because "it's not the same as teaching your class." His solution is to present a lesson that he has done many times before on limericks. In fact, he first taught this lesson while still a student teacher and he remembers that it got a good evaluation from his university supervisor 18 years earlier. On the day of his presentation, he begins by identifying the relevant language arts standards, and then demonstrates the lesson. After he has belabored the rhyme pattern of limericks a bit and shared three examples, one of his colleagues in the audience, pretending to be a slightly obnoxious middle schooler, asks, "Mr. S, do we *have* to write our limericks that way?" and the teacher replies, "No, you can write your poem any way you want." The group falls silent and is left to wonder how a poem can be a limerick if it does not follow a pattern.

The second lesson of the day is an even more mystifying presentation about weather systems, using a mildewed chart. The teacher is obviously uncomfortable when the questions that follow make it clear that even a group of professional educators could not get his point.

Next year, the teachers vote to bring the motivational speaker back.

The intentions of this superintendent and principal may have been good, but the results here were disappointing for all concerned. Putting a solitary teacher on the spot served only to embarrass, intimidate, and reinforce a competitive approach. These two teachers were humiliated in front of colleagues rather than supported by them. The predictable outcome of wounded self-esteem is for the teacher in question to withdraw further rather than seek support through networks of colleagues. In their study of 16 reform networks, Lieberman and Grolnick (1996) defined the concept of a network as including five key ingredients: (1) a strong sense of commitment to innovation; (2) a sense of shared purpose; (3) a mixture of information sharing and psychological support; (4) an effective facilitator; and (5) voluntary participation and equal treatment. The inservice series failed to improve teaching because it failed on all five counts. This story illustrates that even vastly experienced teachers need to revisit planning processes. Professional development activities that focus on planning need to be relevant, effective, continuous, and valued by the administration. Such activities should build interprofessional relationships, not degrade them.

In many ways, the expectations for classroom teachers are the inverse of their realities. Novices are expected to generate elaborate lesson plans and articulate teaching philosophies at a time when most of them are least well equipped to do so. Ironically, after teachers have amassed classroom experience, the assumption is that they no longer need support in lesson design or review, and it is often the case that no one cares to hear the answer to that question that is a standard part of the initial interview, "What is your philosophy of teaching?" Experienced teachers soon learn to keep any misgivings to themselves and to avoid troubling anyone else at school with concerns about teaching effectiveness.

Even when professional development is marginally effective, it tends to gloss over teachers' needs for the right thing at the right time. Virtually every teacher has endured "canned" presentations that disregard the particular teaching circumstances of participants, ignore lesson design, neglect the implementation in classrooms, and skip over peer review of lesson effectiveness. Based on her extensive work in furthering the professional development of teachers in science, mathematics, and technology, the late Susan Loucks-Horsley (2000) concluded:

> Fragmentation plagues current learning opportunities for teachers: courses, workshops, and institutes are rarely coordinated or sustained over time so that teachers get both breadth and depth in what they need to know and be able to do. Long-term professional development programs, not just events, are required to support the kinds of changes required. (p. 32)

From this perspective, effective professional development for teachers must enable them to

- Learn about and acquire new skills
- Deepen content knowledge
- Combine content knowledge with what they know about learning and teaching in their particular contexts
- Motivate them to use tools that will contribute to their learning and that of their students
- Inform them about where and how they can continue to learn

It is also an important way for teachers' practical/professional knowledge to be recognized, expanded, and put to use in mentoring the next generation of teachers. Perhaps most important, participating in research lessons deals in the very sort of "puzzles of practice" (Ershler, 2001) that captivate teachers and hold the greatest promise for promoting teacher learning.

Work with experienced teachers demands an inquiry stance that assumes that teachers' ability to plan is situated (i.e., learner-specific and context-specific), social (i.e., combines individual reflection with group support), and distributed (i.e., different teachers know more or less about some things than others) (Cochran-Smith & Lytle, 2002; Putnam & Borko, 2000; Stokes, 2001). Collaborative planning is closer to teachers' daily practice because it represents an interface between collaborative inquiry and a learning community (Butler, Lauscher, Jarvis-Selinger, & Beckingham, 2004).

Nevertheless, it is not enough to throw teachers together and direct them to work on lessons. First of all, teachers may need coaching in the skills of colleagueship (Minnett, 2003). Accomplishing the goal of collaborative planning demands a departure from the traditional work patterns that reinforce teachers' single-handed planning and implementation of lessons (Kärräinen, 2000). To illustrate how to make the most of inservice teachers' collaborative planning time, consider the experience of a group of teachers who participated in a grant to improve their teaching of American history. One very important piece of the grant was a summer component that included a 3-day workshop for all teachers in grades 4–12 who taught American history and any specialist (art, music, library, special education, technology) who chose to participate. This strategy put teachers together with others who could support their efforts. The workshop also included presentations by university faculty members on the content of history that the teachers would be teaching in the upcoming year, thereby connecting classroom teachers with college instructors. After the presentations, teachers divided into groups to work on the collaborative writing of lesson plans. Group members included teachers at various grade levels and the special-subject teachers. At the end of the workshop, an informal survey was administered so that teachers could share their thoughts on the value and barriers of the 3-day seminar. Survey questions and teachers' responses are as follows:

1. *Briefly explain the collaborative lesson-planning process that you experienced during these workshops.* In response, teachers explained the composition of their groups. For the presentations by university faculty, groups were mixed elementary, secondary, and special-subject teachers. After the initial presentation by the university professors, the groups divided into smaller work groups that were more elementary- or secondary-level-oriented, with support from the specialists.
2. *What did you accomplish during the lesson-planning session?* The number of lesson plans that were completed during the planning session varied from three to six. Lesson topics included the Great Depression, Dust Bowl, explorers, supply and demand, and the Great Compromise. A few teachers commented that they also were able to create supplemental materials such as graphic organizers, rubrics, games, worksheets, and assessments.
3. *What benefits did you experience from this, and other, collaborative planning efforts?* One teacher commented, "The creation of the plan became a 'labor of love' because we share common ideas and philosophies."

Another stated that this experience "raised numerous questions/ ideas that I could not have done on my own." Several teachers commented on the benefits of working with specialists, including making adaptations for students who receive learning support, incorporating music and role-playing into the lessons, and involving the librarian to help with research and resources. The specialists also noted the value of collaboration. One music teacher stated, "I also was able to use a brainstorm idea from a classroom teacher (language arts) to develop a performance-based lesson plan (Cool!)." Several of the participants noted the value of the university professors' expertise in content and resources available that could be shared by the university and school district. One elementary teacher remarked, "We were able to create an excellent document integrating multiple styles of learning." Another wrote, "It is always great to work with other teachers. Everyone has terrific ideas and the end product is normally exceptional."

4. *Were there any barriers during your planning process? If yes, please describe them.* The majority of the respondents did not identify any barriers to the process; however, as mentioned in Chapter 3, power struggles sometimes can be an issue with collaborative planning. Several members of one particular group noted the frustrations of working with a group member who was "controlling," "fussy," and "obsessive." One person added that many times they had to "bow to her whims." The teachers mentioned the importance of having a "give and take" relationship with colleagues and making sure the process worked efficiently and effectively.

   Another group tried to begin the planning process with a large group of mixed elementary, secondary, and special-subject teachers. Later they broke into smaller groups of four or five participants and noted the value of working in smaller work groups to complete the lesson plans.

5. *Will your teaching (either content or pedagogy) change at all as a result of your collaborative planning? If yes, how will it change?* Several teachers mentioned the value of having the university professor go in-depth with content to help the public school teachers have a better background and understanding of history. One secondary teacher mentioned the benefit of having "new lesson plans for new topics." Several teachers mentioned that they now plan to utilize cross-curricular methods by incorporating music, technology, writing, research, and role-playing into their history lessons. A few elementary teachers mentioned that they plan to incorporate more history into their language arts lessons. One secondary teacher planned to change her pedagogy to give students "more responsibility in the learning

process." A learning-support teacher stated that she hopes to be able to be a "more worthwhile support within the history classroom when implementing the lessons."

6. *Please add any additional comments that you would like to make regarding collaborative lesson design.* Comments included, "Collaborative lesson planning is essential for outstanding instruction," "Collaborative lesson design is vital to the continuing growth and development of a professional," and "I can't imagine learning and teaching new curriculum without collaborating with colleagues." Also mentioned was the value of having "critical and immediate feedback." One elementary teacher noted that "divergent thinking and a broader knowledge base certainly enrich lessons created in a collaborative design." Another participant mentioned the benefit of getting a "better grasp of what is needed at upper and lower grade levels."

In addition to the academic value of planning, one secondary history teacher commented that the "esprit de corps, friendships, and meeting new co-workers made it more fun!" Several teachers commented on the overall positive experience and encouraged the district to give teachers more time to work collaboratively to design exceptional lessons for their students.

As these comments from participants amply illustrate, teachers need time to plan with the right people; not only with other teachers, but also with aides, librarians, and other adults who support the learning process (Whelan, 2004). In short, they need to build and participate in learning communities (Mitchell & Sackney, 2001). Building a community of learners (Sergiovanni, 1994; Shields, 2000) depends on three "modes of capacity" (Mitchell & Sackney, 2001).

- *Personal capacity* involves individual teachers confronting and perhaps reconstructing the structures of personal narratives that shape their practice: embedded values, assumptions, beliefs, and practical knowledge. This internal search is complemented by external search-and-questioning processes directed at the various networks (students, colleagues, and community) and professional narratives within which teachers move toward mastery.
- *Interpersonal capacity* depends on fostering both an affective climate where teachers feel affirmed and motivated to participate, and a cognitive climate that encourages learning.
- *Organizational capacity* depends on the productive rearrangement of structures (resources, power relationships, and work design) that can enable and encourage collective learning.

What external forces affect teachers' motivation and freedom to learn what they consider most valuable for their professional practice? What cultural norms and values in their school may be directing their learning in ways they find unproductive? Much of the literature on teacher professional development approaches it from a quality circle/teacher inquiry point of view (Eaker, Dufour, & Burnett, 2002; Gagnon, Collay, Dunlap, & Enloe, 1998; Lieberman & Miller, 2001; Sweeney, 2003). Professional development initiatives thrive where there is a collaborative culture of caring, reciprocal trust and respect, and where the excitement about learning is already well established (Maynes, Knight, McIntosh, & Umpleby, 1995).

PLANNING IN WAYS THAT SUPPORT EXPERTISE

"Think back for a moment on your undergraduate days. Remember when the mysteries of the lesson plan seemed unfathomable?" The question elicited knowing looks and amused smiles from a group of 22 experienced teachers. "Do you think that the format of those plans had been researched thoroughly and was based on empirical evidence?" Most concurred that it was more tradition than research. "What about teachers' manuals? Are they research-based? Who writes them?" "It isn't a teacher!" one teacher offers, and laughter fills the room. "So, you are no longer newcomers to planning, and the teachers' manuals aren't that much help. How do you plan? What do your plans look like?" One teacher says that her plans look like running lists and she crosses off each lesson after it is finished; that way, if she does not get as far as she'd anticipated, there's no need to rewrite. Another says, "They are all in my head. I don't need to write anything down." Someone else comments, "The school provides lesson plan books and I write just enough in each space for a substitute to figure it out." "Does anyone read your plans or comment on them?" Some say that their building principals check to see that plans are submitted weekly. Others say that they are spot-checked by a curriculum supervisor. Several mention that they are expected to include exemplary plans in their professional portfolio.

We contend that at least five research-based recommendations must be met in order to improve the planning processes of experienced teachers: (1) articulation of theories, (2) attention to lesson design that matches goals to strategies, (3) making good choices, (4) teaching for understanding, and (5) lesson-focused reflection.

Articulation of Theories

As Wilson and Wineburg (1991) discuss in their study of history teachers, a group of practitioners may, at any point, hold diverse beliefs about knowledge, pedagogical content knowledge, instructional methods and strategies, curriculum, theories of learning, and the respective roles and responsibilities of pupils and teachers. There is growing evidence that when teachers articulate their theories and align them with instructional practice, student achievement is improved (Jinkins, 2001; Levande; 1988; Mastrini-McAteer, 1997). Latching onto "what works" (Shannon, 2000), without much attention to why or how, often compromises the learning process. "Teachers may gain understandings of a specific strategy or process and fail to see the connections between and among them that result in more effective practice. Through continuous feedback and engagement these connections are established and maintained" (Jinkins, 2001, p. 283). What is commonly lacking in lesson planning is a deliberate effort to orient or design instruction around the actual process of learning, as expressed in theories.

Attention to Lesson Design

Actually, what most educators refer to as lesson planning emphasizes the delivery of the lesson, not the design. Lesson design emphasizes opportunities for students to make connections between new information and their existing cognitive structures (Panasuk, Stone, & Todd, 2002). One model for lesson design is the Four Stages of Lesson Planning. The goal of this model for lesson planning in mathematics is to help teachers in their process of organizing for instruction. It begins with goals for the students (objectives), then moves to desired performance outcomes (homework), next to activities that will enable students to independently complete the homework (developmental activities), and finally to the underlying understandings necessary to complete each task along the way (mental mathematics)(Panasuk, Stone, & Todd, 2002). Note that the sequence is very different from the one used to deliver lessons, which would be: objectives, developmental activities, mental mathematics, and homework. The reason for approaching lesson design using the identical components used in lesson delivery, but in a different sequence, is that it results in more coherent structure and serves to integrate each lesson and align lesson goals with instructional strategies. It is also, in the estimation of these math experts, better suited to the specific content area of mathematics.

Making Good Choices

Most of us have heard (or perhaps recall saying it ourselves) that familiar wail from teachers, "Just tell us what to do!" Today that cry has been answered with a vengeance, as standards, tests, and prepared curricula dominate the educational scene. All of these materials are long on telling teachers what to do and short on how to achieve results. Telling is the easy part. Saying how is exceedingly difficult. Even when working with a prepared curriculum, teachers make many decisions about such things as what parts of the teachers' guide to read, what purposes to emphasize, which of the suggested activities to do, how to structure lessons, and ways to respond to the students (Ashby, Lee, & Shemilt, 2005; Remillard, 1999, 2000; Remillard & Geist, 2002). As Davis and Sumara (1997) have argued, a teacher's intentions for practice, perceptions about the changing self, perceptions about what counts as valuable knowledge, language for articulating these perceptions, and everyday choices and responses cannot be understood in isolation from the organization's cultural and physical environment.

Teaching for Understanding

Many students experience difficulty when applying their knowledge and skills because the knowledge and skills are taught, at best, in fragmented, isolated, and mechanical ways. Collaborative planning is associated not only with stronger patterns of achievement in students but also with higher levels of concept development (Hiebert & Stigler, 2000). When the goal is to teach for understanding, it is more productive to develop an analysis of the mental process by which new concepts are acquired than to ask students to imitate a teacher's behavior or listen to a lecture. While it is the students' responsibility to construct knowledge, this does not suggest a laissez-faire approach on the part of teachers. Rather, students rely on experts who construct "pre-disposing structures and influences" that explain and illustrate everything necessary to support learners' cognitive development (Stiff, 2000, p. 812). Teaching for understanding requires experienced teachers to move beyond attention to materials and procedures and link them with concepts. In her study, Ma (1999) describes how Chinese teachers treat knowledge like "packages" in which the concepts and skills are related. The packages differ somewhat from one teacher to the next, but the contents are much the same. "Procedural knowledge and skills need to be *organized around core concepts*" (Donovan & Bransford, 2005, p. 19, emphasis in original).

Lesson-Focused Reflection

Teaching concepts could be improved if each teacher asked three questions on a regular basis: (1) Where am I now? (in terms of the knowledge children in the classroom have available to build upon); (2) Where do I want to go? (in terms of the knowledge he or she wants all children in the classroom to acquire during the school year); and (3) What is the best way to get there? (in terms of the learning opportunities he or she will provide to enable all children in the class to reach the chosen objectives) (Griffin, 2005). Answers to such challenging questions often are better formulated when teachers can address them together. This is the premise of collaborative lesson review.

Wilms (2003), who worked with a lesson study in Los Angeles, found that elementary and secondary teachers were unanimously supportive of the lesson-study process. The teachers' evaluations of lesson study emphasized the value of collaboration, improving teacher quality, helping students to learn, promoting leadership in the school and district, using time more effectively, fostering better classroom management, and building administrative support. In addition, research suggests that different types of pedagogical content knowledge and concerns are apt to flourish in different contexts (De Jong, 2000). A teacher may, for example, be more willing to discuss concerns about his or her personal ability to fulfill the teacher's role on an individual basis and more willing to discuss task concerns in a group.

THE ROLE OF TEACHER PROFESSIONAL GROWTH PLANS

One way in which administrators can demonstrate their commitment to effective planning is by making it an integral part of teachers' professional growth plans. A study in Alberta, Canada, described how groups of teachers engaged in "patient dialogue" and "deep talk" about professional practice that provided a rare opportunity to build a "culture of conversation about learning" (Fenwick, 2004, p. 272). The challenges of implementing teacher professional growth plans were similar to those encountered by schools seeking to implement other forms of teacher collaboration, namely:

- To affirm personal capacity, permit flexibility, provide incentives, and encourage accountability for learning in teachers without exercising control through hierarchical power relationships

- To identify approaches that had a positive impact on students' learning while, at the same time, honoring teachers as self-directed professionals who possess different needs and learning processes
- To allocate resources in ways that supported meaningful teacher learning even when demands overwhelmed the time available and a higher priority was attached to lesson delivery than to other stages in the teaching/learning process (Fenwick, 2004)

The Teacher Professional Growth Plan in Alberta sheds light on an element that often is missing in the collaborative planning projects implemented in many schools: external guidance. In our experience, it is common for administrators to go to extremes. They may "give" teachers time and step away, hoping for the best, or they may "use" collaboration as a smokescreen for surveillance. In the former, teachers soon realize that the activity is not truly valued by the administration based on apparent disinterest in the outcome; in the latter, teachers quickly determine that what the administration really wants is uniformity and compliance. In both cases, the results are paltry and the innovation is abandoned as soon as any other external pressure impinges on it. A middle ground would offer administrative guidance that would encourage wider participation in the activity, assist teachers in arriving at a manageable plan, and provide external validation of teachers' efforts, progress, and professional accomplishments. Balancing internal guidance (teacher reflection) with external guidance (administrative support) is the most powerful combination.

CONCLUSION: PLANNING AS PROFESSIONAL DEVELOPMENT

Collaborative lesson design, planning, delivery, and review are key to promoting professional development because they support experienced teachers' efforts in four domains.

1. *Acquiring self-efficacy,* which occurs when teachers believe that they can exert a powerful, positive influence on students' learning; hold high expectations that all children can learn, develop, and grow; influence respected colleagues and make a contribution to the class, program, grade level, school, or system; and have confidence that they can enlist the support of parents/families/communities to mobilize resources and achieve important goals. Teaching a concept with limited success can lead to frustration and, over time, teachers can begin to lower

their expectations for students and dilute the curriculum. Collaborative planning efforts build teachers' sense of efficacy by suggesting more effective alternatives.

2. *Developing greater competence,* which occurs when teachers increase their knowledge of content (terminology, facts, concepts, and basic principles) of various disciplines; enhance their pedagogical expertise; expand their repertoires of specific teaching strategies; acquire the skills of collaboration and put them to use in improving the curriculum; and work in a culture that recognizes excellence.

3. *Moving closer to democratic ideals,* which occurs when teachers engage in principled practices in all interactions with children, families, community members, and colleagues; advocate for social justice in schools and larger communities; use ethical reasoning to address concerns, analyze issues, and solve problems; and recognize that their responsibility to teach extends to all students irrespective of their socioeconomic status, levels of parental support for learning, and prior learning experiences.

4. *Becoming members of a collegial community,* which occurs when teachers belong to a group of trusted and admired professionals who can offer advice and support; are respected by colleagues who are held in high esteem; know how to gain the attention, support, and participation of colleagues in pursuing worthwhile goals; contribute to the development of the next generation of teachers; and extend their sphere of influence beyond the immediate environment to other educators in the field (Jalongo & Isenberg, 2004).

A college professor was meeting with three principals to discuss a presentation for parents at the school she had attended as a child 35 years earlier. During the course of their conversation, the administrators mentioned to the professor that she might recall Miss Burkett, one of the teachers from the school, who was going to retire. The professor did recall Miss Burkett, and fondly. Across an elementary school career, she was the only teacher who had visited their family's home. Miss Burkett was loved and respected equally by parents and children, and her name was remembered instantly, after other teachers' names had been long forgotten. The school administrators reported that Miss Burkett's career had spanned 49 years and her effectiveness had not diminished in the least.

Such "super teachers" who work tirelessly and have found their own ways of supporting professional growth, while remarkable, are not commonplace. Education needs to draw inspiration from their stories, yes, but it has a larger obligation to invest in the professional growth and development of all practicing teachers in ways that enable them to truly benefit from experience.

CHAPTER 5

Planning and Professional Expertise: Teaching to a Higher Standard

Adoctoral program applicant had just completed a brief research-based presentation to six faculty members. The applicant had chosen No Child Left Behind legislation as her topic, and although she had not stated it plainly, there was an undercurrent of criticism in her remarks. During the discussion that followed, one professor asked, "If you and other educators share dissatisfaction with schools, why don't teachers rise up or speak out?" The prospective student responded solemnly, "Because resistance is futile." Her reply alluded to a group of beings called the Borg from the television program *Star Trek: The Next Generation.* The Borg used mind control to maintain order in their society and to dominate other species. Although some may object to the analogy, it appears that, in much the same way that the launching of Sputnik in 1957 spurred the United States to concentrate on science and mathematics in schools, the fact that American students failed to place first in international comparisons has raised concerns about the nation's ability to maintain world economic superiority.

In response, the federal government has turned to state academic standards, state testing programs, a focus on narrow empirical findings, and harsh consequences (i.e., replacing teachers, closing schools, withholding funds, support for private schools) as a strategy for controlling public education (Chapman, 2004). Here the pressure is on teachers to wring higher and higher scores out of students; any other course of action risks watching their schools placed on the endangered list and perhaps dismantled. Yet, as Cunningham and Creamer (2003) contend, top-down edicts fall far short of the mark. Only a competent instructional staff can bring efforts to improve public education to fruition.

Too many professors of education, employees of state departments of public instruction, employees of central offices in school districts, and public school principals insist on maintaining the current accountability system in some form. Why? Because they do not have to know how to do anything except how to threaten and cajole teachers into "increasing achievement.". . . In the best practices mode, they would actually have to know what those best practices were and how to support and guide teachers' implementation of those best practices in classrooms. It is much easier to use, or advocate the use of, carrots and sticks to get teachers to try harder to do what you could not do yourself. (p. 336)

There is little doubt that threatening a public school with extinction or a postsecondary institution with loss of accreditation affects the thoughts and behaviors of educators and teacher educators. The important question is whether the imposition of that power has positive outcomes for education. Many leaders in the field think it does not. As Deborah Meier (2003) observes:

The current focus on testing calls for a curriculum that is an inch deep and a mile wide, a curriculum that aims at rote learning, and a pedagogy that focuses on coverage and right answers. Its virtues are simplicity, alignment, measurability. . . . Getting to the wrong place faster, however, is not a virtue. (p. 16)

The standards movement appears to be pushing educators at all levels, from preschool through graduate school, to follow unquestioningly, substitute public policy for philosophy, and prefer the quantitative over the qualitative.

This tail called the test is wagging the proverbial dog in higher education as well. Recently we asked a group of 18 experienced classroom teachers who aspire to become college faculty a question about assessment on an exam. All were acutely aware of the state-mandated tests that decide the fate of elementary and secondary schools; none were familiar with assessment practices in higher education, and most admitted that any thoughts they had on the matter were based on personal recollections from their undergraduate days. These 18 teachers assumed that higher education was somehow exempt from testing pressures. What few public school personnel realize is that the Educational Testing Service has assumed an unprecedented level of importance in colleges of education as tests to assess each stage and area of certification are published. This reliance on national test data, coupled with the pressures of accreditation agencies such as the National Council for the Accreditation of Teacher Education, has exerted considerable pressure on teacher educators. It is no longer sufficient to show that preservice and inservice teachers have acquired subject-matter competence; colleges of education now have to demonstrate that their current students are becoming (and their program graduates have become) competent and effective professionals. College of education faculty and administrators celebrate when Praxis scores are high and panic when they are low. In colleges and universities, it is increasingly common to see thick practice books, cram sessions, and short courses for students who are preparing to take the Praxis or have already failed the test.

In the early 21st century, educators at all levels anxiously anticipate the test summary data, not because they will use the information to improve the curriculum but because they intend to teach to the test. Sadly, the mantle of scientific research has been conferred upon easy-to-score, multiple-choice tests; they have attained a status far above their original station in life and have become the operational definition of instructional effectiveness. If the situation sounds desperate, it is. Little wonder, then, that one professional development day with a visiting expert, no matter how charismatic and competent, does little more than send a mixed message to teachers. Everyone knows that standardized tests now are the metronome to which the soundtrack of modern education is paced. In these difficult and uncertain educational times, neither large-group, one-shot professional development nor the excellence of a few good teachers will suffice. The critical mass of teachers and teacher educators will have to function as scholars, leaders, and colleagues if resistance is to be anything more than futile.

TEACHERS AS SCHOLARS:
PROMOTING RESEARCH-BASED PRACTICE

Teachers' educational attainment in the United States has risen dramatically. Many teachers of the 1800s would be barely literate by today's standards and would be stymied by the tests administered to contemporary 4th graders. Expectations for teachers have risen as well. Nevertheless, as Farley (2001) points out:

> In one hundred years, we have gone from the intimate instruction of the little red schoolhouse to the impersonal pedagogy of the big brown school factory. Few attempts to reinvent have arisen from educational research, and shame on us for that. We have been too much the compliant technocrats serving the system. (p. 76)

A group of 34 experienced teachers worked in small groups and generated a list of impediments to using research to guide their professional practice. During the large-group discussion afterwards, they identified numerous barriers, which we summarize here:

- Researchers could be devious and dishonest or might misrepresent the data accidentally; not all research can be trusted.

- Some research has little to say about practical issues. It raises an issue but stops short of a solution.
- Teachers do not have the time, the inclination, and, at times, the research expertise to read lengthy, complicated research reports.
- The link between the study results and implications for practice is not always clear, and results may conflict with teachers' practical knowledge.
- Results from one study sometimes contradict those from another.
- The limitations of the study sometimes make the results of studies seem obvious or trivial.
- Teachers' limited knowledge of research designs and methods make it difficult to determine if the study was of high quality.

Bringing all of these reservations to light seemed like a strange way to conclude the first class meeting of a required research course. The instructor followed with this question: "Suppose that I told you about instructional strategies that have improved students' comprehension of written text. The strategies have been used with learners at different grade levels from elementary school through community college and each strategy has been supported by multiple studies. Would you try them?" Most of the teachers appeared eager to know what these strategies were, but they would have to wait until the next class meeting to find out (Block & Pressley, 2001). The class was kept in suspense quite deliberately to encourage them to wonder what applied research in literacy has to say to them as teachers.

As this example serves to illustrate, education has to move beyond the consciousness-raising stage of bemoaning the rift between research and practice. More pertinent questions about the effects of research on classroom teaching are:

- What counts as research and why? Who says so?
- What types of educational research have the most to say to practitioners?
- At what point in the teaching/learning cycle is research most applicable?
- How do teachers go about applying research findings?

Although it is taken for granted that the results of research ought to be directly applied by teachers in the classroom, this assumption is decidedly problematic (Fenstermacher, 1994). Basic research is too far removed from implications for practice to offer much guidance, and the primary purpose of many other studies is to identify problems, not to solve them. Actually, it is applied research, particularly research that attempts to evaluate the relative effectiveness of various instructional materials, strategies, procedures, and plans, that has the most direct bearing on classroom instruction (Farstrup & Samuels, 2002).

The current scene is dominated by calls for "scientific research," narrowly defined as quantitative, quasi-experimental studies. This push is strongest in the content area that is valued above all others in U.S. society and education, namely, literacy. What frequently is overlooked in discussions of "evidence-based literacy instruction" is that research has the most to say, not during lesson delivery, but during lesson design. If lesson planning can be conceptualized as a cycle that begins with lesson design; moves to planning, then to implementation, and next to review of the learners' responses; and finally comes full circle to lesson redesign (see Figure 5.1), then applications of research would tend to be of most value early and late in the planning cycle, in other words, during lesson design and redesign. Our contention is that proponents of evidence-based instruction bring educational research into the mix far too late to be of much value because their narrow view of what counts as teaching is limited to standing in front of the classroom, delivering a body of content, and rehearsing for the test.

Figure 5.1 Lesson-Planning Cycle

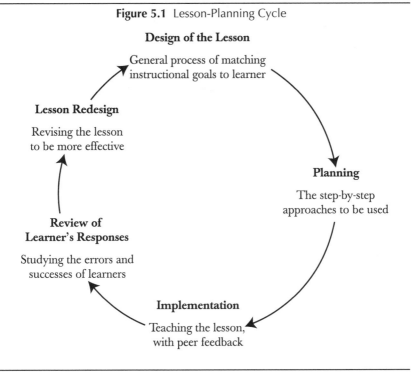

Just as what is tested gets taught to learners, what is supported by school systems gets accomplished by teachers. If schools continue to marginalize teacher planning processes and treat them as "outside" of real teaching, then it is to be expected that teachers will concentrate on the things that (apparently) matter most in the bureaucracy called school. Teachers quickly ascertain that the best way to ensure their continued employment is to maintain order in the classroom, prepare students for the test, and follow increasingly prescriptive teachers' manuals. Of course, if teachers do this, education will not improve because, in this scenario, teachers are mindless functionaries of the system.

What discussions of evidence-based instruction tend to ignore are the efforts to synthesize research that conflicts with the behavioristic political agendas. Farstrup and Samuels (2002) warn that

> Research is most influential when its findings match the social, political, and economic tenor of the times. Studies that demonstrate something that the field or society wants to believe at a given moment are the ones that will be most influential. Research matters most not necessarily when it provides the best or most accurate answers, but when it offers the answers that we most want to hear. (p. 20)

Based on a review of research, Zemelman, Daniels, and Hyde (1998), for example, identified the 12 research-based principles of effective instructional practices shown in Figure 5.2.

Figure 5.2 Research-Based Principles of Effective Teaching and Learning

In general, effective teaching/learning experiences are:

1. Student-centered (based on learners' interests),
2. Experiential (involving learners in active, hands-on, concrete activities),
3. Holistic (emphasizing whole events and processes rather than drill on sub-parts),
4. Authentic (providing real, rich, complex ideas),
5. Reflective (encouraging learners to analyze thoughts and feelings),
6. Social (offering opportunities for interpersonal interaction),
7. Collaborative (encouraging cooperative approaches),
8. Democratic (establishing communities founded on social justice)
9. Cognitive (involving learners in applying higher-order thinking skills),
10. Developmental (suited to the child's level),
11. Constructivist (respecting the learner's need to reinvent and reconstruct information in personally meaningful ways), and
12. Challenging (offering genuine challenges and choices, and promoting responsibility).

Source: Zemelman, Daniels, & Hyde, 1998

The loudest voices for scientific research and evidence-based instruction consider only narrow empirical efforts that yield one-liner results that are used to stoke the steam engine of the quick-fix, back-to-basics train. Teachers and teacher educators need to know the research themselves to avoid being bullied by those who pretend to know it. This is not as daunting a task as it may seem. To illustrate, we used a meta-analysis of the research on K–4 reading instruction to identify 11 different research-supported strategies (Greenwood, Tapia, Abbott, & Walton, 2003). The list included: (1) shared book experience, (2) phonemic awareness activities, (3) repeated reading, (4) initial reading blending, (5) early intervention reading, (6) partner reading, (7) word family books, (8) Dolch sight word list, (9) peer tutoring in reading, (10) peer tutoring in spelling, (11) partner reading questions, and (12) reciprocal teaching. We told a group of 34 experienced elementary school teachers pursuing their M.Ed. that we would be checking their familiarity with research-based reading strategies, and they seemed a bit uncomfortable at the prospect of being tested in this way. Yet after the list was distributed, their faces relaxed and every teacher was well acquainted with just about every item on the list; nearly all reported using the strategies while teaching. Nevertheless, these teachers had been so beaten down by vague calls for "evidence-based reading instruction" at school that they *expected* to be ignorant of the strategies. They needed to trust what they already knew. Unless and until teachers work together to move away from slapdash lesson plans and learn to articulate that they are, indeed, drawing upon research during the lesson-planning process, they will remain vulnerable to being controlled and intimidated by someone else's insistence on data-driven teaching.

TEACHERS AS LEADERS: RECLAIMING CONSTRUCTIVISM

Over 15 years ago, William Glasser (1990) captured the difficult situation that many teachers confront today.

> Most competent teachers recognize . . . that the effort to stuff students with measurable fragments of knowledge has little or nothing to do with high-quality education. . . . If they teach conceptually and challenge students to think and defend their ideas, the students will have a chance to learn something worthwhile. But, since the students may not do well on tests that measure fragments, such teachers will be labeled as troublemakers and failures. On the other hand, if they teach the way they are told to teach, the students will fail to learn anything that the students believe is worthwhile. But their teachers will be praised as successful team players, and the students will be blamed as incompetent. There is always the fear in education,

especially among the measurers and fragmenters, that too great a concern with quality means that students inevitably cover less ground. The opposite occurs: quality always leads to increased productivity. (p. 430)

The forum in which that quality and productivity emerge is not the teachers' lounge, not a 15-minute planning period shared by no one else, and not the one-shot professional development session led by a visiting expert. Lessons are the place. Lessons are also the place where teacher interest is understandably high, consultants' knowledge is often limited, and sharing an effective lesson can increase its impact exponentially beyond a single classroom.

This century began with bright hopes that education was moving toward a constructivist philosophy. From this perspective, knowledge is "constructed individually and socially rather than being objective and separate from the knower" (McCutcheon & Milner, 2002, pp. 89–90). The implementation of a constructivist philosophy is not without its challenges, however. Whelan (2004) analyzed an extended, interdisciplinary unit in social studies that was based on the principles of constructivism. The culminating project was a history museum that middle school students designed and installed in the local town hall. Reflecting on this successful project, the researcher concluded that such projects demand a level of planning from teachers that is far from typical.

Planning assignments that require students to construct meaning for themselves is more complicated than planning more traditional, teacher-centered instruction. That explains why teacher-centered instruction remains so prevalent, despite such longstanding, well-founded criticism of its effectiveness. That type of instruction is easier to plan, requiring in most cases that teachers plan for themselves alone . . . [conversely] a single teacher cannot do all that is necessary to organize and monitor a full class of students working individually or in small groups on activities that require them to construct meaning for themselves and to share that meaning among themselves and with a wider audience. Other adults need to be involved, and that involvement invariably requires additional planning. (p. 56)

Today, an information-dispensing approach to lesson planning has overtaken schools in a tsunami-like wave of accountability. It is the very antithesis of constructivism because it blithely treats knowledge and curriculum as if they were "objective and value neutral" and treats teaching as if it were "transmitted directly from the teacher or textbook to the students" (McCutcheon & Milner, 2002, pp. 89–90). Only the rare teacher can stand alone against such powerful political and social forces. Collaborative planning is a way of calling out to all educators to embrace the curriculum leadership role. This recommendation runs counter to much of what teachers have learned along the way. As Wilcox (2002) points out, "Many teachers who emerge as leaders try to keep a low profile. After all, aren't teachers supposed to be followers? Doesn't taking a leadership role make one's peers look bad? Where in teacher preparation programs are leadership skills taught?" (p. 3). As we have argued throughout this book, collaborative lesson-planning strategies represent a leadership-friendly approach that can be taught to teacher candidates as part of their teacher preparation programs. Collaborative planning also merits cultivation in practicing teachers through a wide range of professional development activities such as inservice training, teacher networks, and graduate study. The goal would be for educators at all levels to regard leadership as fundamental to effective teaching.

> The success of professional development is dependent on several factors: eagerness to learn from a variety of sources, responsible preparation for entering our educational debates, openness to well-considered change, and willingness to look foolish while learning new strategies. I cannot ask my students to take intellectual risks if I fail to model with them the joys and the struggles inherent in learning and living. (Smith, 2003, p. 4)

To reclaim constructivism is to make an enduring commitment to student learning, to one's own learning, and to that of colleagues and the larger community.

TEACHERS AS COLLEAGUES: FROM ACCOUNTABILITY TO RESPONSIBILITY

Colleagues in education are individuals who accept personal responsibility for their actions and, at the same time, share a commitment to the learners and to one another in ways that uphold the principles of social justice. Reflective, growth-oriented models of learning that rely on dialogue and relationships, and are founded upon trust and mutual respect, tend to increase collegiality (McBride & Skau, 1995; Poole, 1995). As Whelan (2004) explains:

> Accountability is essentially extrinsic in nature, with its focus of answerability fixed on some externally defined set of objectives and implying some externally imposed consequences for shortcomings. Responsibility is much the opposite in both respects, with an implicit sense of allegiance and obligation arising from an internalized set of principled understandings about what it means to lead a good human life. . . .

> Responsibility, in other words, is a goal more consistent with school-ing's longstanding citizenship purposes. Those purposes are inclusive of the narrower vision of schooling that the standards-based and student-ac-countability movement represents but entail a much fuller and more en-nobling sense of what it means to be an active participant in a society ever striving to further itself as a political and social democracy. (p. 61)

Political and social obstacles to colleagueship in U.S. schools are formi-dable, not the least of which is blind faith in the salutary effects of capital-ism, free enterprise, and individual striving. Carlgren (1999) analyzes the situation in her native country of Sweden in ways that ring true for U.S. educators, as summarized here.

1. Unlike traditional crafts or other professions, teachers' pro-fessional knowledge is looked upon as nonexistent or even "wrong." "When physicians say they cannot cure a certain form of cancer, nobody doubts it. If teachers say they cannot teach certain things to certain children, teachers are considered to be in need of further education" (Carlgren, 1999, p. 48). This makes it difficult to accumulate knowledge and diminishes re-spect for teachers.

2. There is a contradiction between teachers' knowledge and new demands such that "teachers' work is characterized by rup-tures rather than continuities" (p. 44). Implicit in each reform is a loss of competence from the teachers' point of view as teachers constantly are being asked to do what they have not done before and to perform in ways unsupported by their tacit knowledge.

3. It is not sufficient for teachers to attain higher levels of compe-tence; they also are expected to be "paradigmatically correct," that is, aligned philosophically with the current trends. This makes education a field highly sensitive to fads and fashions. Here we would add that a conflicting paradigm often is a point of friction between basic and higher education. Teachers who are self-described as being "in the trenches" may feel that they are being judged by professors who are too theoretical and out of touch with the realities of the classroom.

4. Much of the current reform effort actually focuses not so much on teachers' work inside the classroom, but on what goes on outside the classroom in the form of lesson design and rede-sign. The very school systems that are demanding this type of work, however, continue to define teaching as contact with

students and relegate anything else to the lowly status of actions performed before (or after) "real" teaching.

Interestingly, Carlgren (1999) reports that her country launched a public relations campaign with the slogan, "Teachers lift Sweden." This is a departure from practice in the United States, where criticism is heaped on public schools and teachers and we can think of no comparable, national, federally supported effort to elevate the professional status of classroom teachers.

Contemporary perspectives on teaching appear to have reverted to the efficiency model perspective that Raymond Callahan (1964) critiqued in the mid-20th century. Imagine that, instead of treating teaching like piecework in a factory, the before- and after-teaching phases attained equal stature with student contact hours. A new metaphor might be that of landscape design. First of all, it is accepted that a landscape architect's work is not confined to the time when the drawing is unveiled to the client; rather, the most time-consuming and important component occurs as the terrain is studied, a theme is chosen, the plan is conceptualized, and the design is transformed into a drawing. This metaphor is far more appropriate than that of the assembly line. Just as the landscape designer's role is not by any means limited to the planting phase, and the measure of its success is the overall effect on the landscape, the act of teaching needs to be connected with the design phase and the lesson review, and with the success of the endeavor for all children.

Professional growth, by definition, takes place at the edge of teachers' competence and performance. Whether it is the yellowed lecture notes of college professors or the tired teaching units of a preschool teacher, there are unfortunate examples of teachers at all levels who have become less, rather than more, skilled with additional years of practice. The term *professional development* should not be applied lightly to any gathering of educators. Becoming an expert teacher requires a dedicated, relentless effort. In the current educational climate, brilliant teaching is still "a subversive activity" of sorts (Postman & Weingartner, 1971), for teachers who make a commitment to social justice in schools and communities (Cochran-Smith, 2004) and reassert that "the democratic mission of schooling" is at the "heart of the educational process" (Westheimer & Kahne, 2003, p. 14) often find themselves at odds with the system.

If we have learned anything from the study of innovation during decades when the buzzwords of education were accountability, reform, and restructuring, it is that top-down directives alone cannot succeed in making substantive improvements in schools. True, a policy may put a new veneer on education, but any enduring improvements in the quality of instruction and learning have made teachers central to the process (Meier, 2002). If the Professional Development School literature has taught us anything, it is that educational reform that focuses exclusively on student achievement, without concomitant attention to the professional growth of classroom teachers and a consideration of college and university faculty who work with teachers, is destined to fail, for it ignores key players involved in the process (Campoy, 2000).

Consider, for example, the Literacy Hour that was legislated in the United Kingdom. Mandating an hour of balanced literacy activities certainly had an effect on the schools; however, as one might anticipate, some teachers decided to follow the letter of the law rather than its spirit. Observational research about the Literacy Hour suggests that, in response to top-down impositions, teachers often adopted "a wait and see" attitude and postponed changes in their teaching until it was clear that the initiative would not fade away (Fisher, 2002). Teachers in the United States are equally weary of the constant clamor for change that often is motivated by political ambition or budgetary considerations rather than a commitment to children and families.

> Most schools still operate along the same lines as the old mass-production facilities. Bells ring, students move through a fragmented curriculum, and the hours fly by. The quality of student learning is measured by narrow tests, and, increasingly, teachers' salaries and school resources are being tied to test scores. Teachers have little time or incentive to work together as professionals in the service of children's learning. Most teachers cope simply by walling themselves off inside their own classrooms and teaching the best that they know how. (Wilms, 2003, p. 608)

It is not until the power of an idea captures the imagination of a critical mass of educators that improvements occur, as was the case with open education, whole language, and performance assessment. Each of these movements respected teachers, and each had some staying power in a field that is notorious for faddism. They flourished where there was administrative support and languished where there was not. One limitation that teachers perceived in these initiatives was that they did not focus squarely on implementation, leaving practitioners to figure it out for themselves.

Collaborative planning holds promise because it gains support from the top for a grassroots movement (Fernandez & Chokshi, 2002). Collaborative planning also actualizes internal reflection by connecting it with a network of teachers (Adams, 2000a) within and across schools and districts. Teacher networks are successful when they

- Deepen subject-matter knowledge

- Lead to greater pedagogical expertise

- Focus on children's learning

- Establish a culture of collaboration

- Develop skill in analyzing professional practice in a safe and supportive context

- Forge connections with other professionals in particular subject areas and in education in general

- Prepare educators to function as leaders and make organizational changes (King & Neumann, 2000; Morris, Chrispeels, & Burke, 2003)

There is little doubt that the standards movement in U.S. education is intended not only to increase student achievement but also to prod teachers to attain higher levels of expertise. What is noticeably absent in the current system is a fundamental understanding of professional expertise in teachers: what it is, how it develops, and ways that the culture of schools must change to support it.

Perhaps most pertinent to any discussion of colleagueship among teachers is an understanding of how an individual practitioner's knowledge contributes to the general professional knowledge base for educators. Hiebert, Gallimore, and Stigler (2002) contend that active participation and reflection are required to transform practical knowledge—which is detailed, concrete, specific, and linked with practice—into a professional knowledge base. An individual teacher's knowledge makes a contribution to the professional knowledge base when it is made public, stored, shared, verified, and improved. Thus, the collaborative lesson is a major way of converting teachers' expertise from a solitary ability into a shared strength. When teachers work in isolation there is little opportunity to make expertise public, to store it systematically, to share it beyond the boundaries of a particular setting, to verify it through the process of peer review, or even to improve upon it through professional dialogue. This begs the question, "If collaborative planning is an appropriate response to the issue of teacher quality, why have teacher-planning processes in the United States tended to be individual, rather than group initiatives?" As we have pointed out in this book, there are many explanations, not the least of which are traditions in the field of education and in school cultures where, increasingly, teachers are graded and compared.

MISCONCEPTIONS ABOUT TEACHER EXPERTISE

A group of college juniors enrolled in a teaching methods course in language arts had just finished watching a video of a student teacher's exemplary kindergarten lesson in an urban classroom. Afterwards, the professor asked if there were any comments or questions. One student who had been struggling throughout her practicum in an elementary school that semester was the first to speak. "She's not really like us, right? I mean, she seems a lot *older*." A few other students agreed, eager to credit chronological age for this teacher's professional poise, effective organization, and ability to keep a large and diverse group of kindergartners fully engaged. The instructor reminded the students that during their earlier discussions in the class, several of them had been quick to associate a *loss* of teacher competence with advancing age. (One student had remarked, "If they are sick and tired of teaching, they should retire and make room for us!"). So, evidently, some of them believed that not all teachers improve with age or experience. After it was established that the student teacher in the video was indeed a traditional-age college senior, a few students insisted that she must have amassed more experience working with children. One commented, "Maybe she worked in child care or at a camp during the summer," and another said, "I'll bet she has children." Students with the least well-developed pedagogical skills seemed determined to attribute the success of the teacher in the videotape to inevitable forces such as advancing age or to experiences extrinsic to school, such as child rearing. Abilities that were more intrinsic and required deliberate effort, such as building knowledge, acquiring pedagogical skill, making a commitment to children and families, engaging in reflective practices, and pursuing professional development, went by unmentioned.

Some preservice teachers persist in the vain hope that they will emerge from their teacher preparation programs as finished products and that, upon graduation, all that will remain is to soak up the "real world" of teaching. Clearly, it's not that easy. For unless teachers engage in, as John Dewey (1910) described it, "reconstructing experience," their capacities are limited almost before they begin and their expertise can be expected to decline with time and experience. Teachers must be learners in order to lead others to learning. As told in the following case study, the experience of a new college-level instructor, Jim Preston, helps to illustrate how such reconstructions can be made part of teacher preparation.

CASE STUDY:
"I THINK THAT, IN LIFE, IDEAS IN ISOLATION ARE LIMITED."

Jim Preston began his college teaching career with a large measure of enthusiasm for collaborative planning processes because, as he put it, "if future teachers start their careers working collaboratively with other future teachers to plan and evaluate lessons, then they will take that habit into the profession." As an experienced secondary mathematics teacher and doctoral candidate, Jim was familiar with the research on Japanese lesson study and sought to adapt it for use in his teaching methods course in secondary mathematics and science. All of the students in his evening class were nontraditional-age college students and mid-career professionals with work lives, families, and a shared commitment to entering the teaching profession. To begin, Jim asked the students this question:

> How do you go about planning a lesson? Please do not describe what you are supposed to do; rather, describe what you actually do. What do you typically do first and why? Next? And so forth.

Students' responses made it clear that they operated rather differently, depending on each student's stage of professional growth and personal/professional styles. One student focused on the information, relying on textbooks and Internet sources and memories as a student, saving the assessment piece for last.

> When planning my lessons, I start by seeing what aspects are covered in the textbook. . . . I also try to recall issues I had when I was first introduced to the topic. Following the recommendations from our textbook, I try to develop ideas for an opening activity that can pull previous and necessary knowledge into the lesson. Then I create an outline for what new information I would like to introduce. . . . Then, I develop a lesson around an activity while supporting the activity with a direct discussion of new terminology or concepts. Next, I look for ways to provide guided practice to model how to solve problems related to the new concept. Lastly, I look for a good homework assignment that will give the students practice.

Another student reported that she started at the end with a review of the unit's scope and assessment and a review of the homework problems: "I try to step back and think about the knowledge a person must have to tackle the homework problems."

A third began with the connections.

> I actually try to develop both the lesson and the associated assess-
> ment together, to make sure that they "match." I have a general
> idea of what I want the students to learn, and then I sketch out
> ways to present that information to the students. I really want stu-
> dents to be able to "connect" to the information I teach by apply-
> ing real-world examples.

Jim respected these differences, yet conceptualized the role of the
teacher educator as that of a change agent and selected "teaching for
understanding" as the unifying theme of the course. Originally, his admittedly ambitious goal was for students to develop several collaborative lesson plans using the lesson study format (Fernandez & Chokshi,
2002; http://www.tc.columbia.edu/lessonstudy/index.html). He soon
realized, however, that

> students were apprehensive with this new process of lesson study.
> After reading the article in class, they saw the value in the process
> but were not as enthusiastic when they were faced with imple-
> menting the process in class. There were a lot of questions. Shortly
> after that class I received an e-mail from a student expressing con-
> cern over the process. The main concern was that less-than-mean-
> ingful criticism would be given because students would not want
> to affect classmates' grades, would fear reprisals if they were can-
> did, or would be overly critical of one another if this deteriorated
> into a competitive process.

Jim decided that "much of this was not possible," given the inexperience
of the group, the time constraints of the class, and his own isolation as an
adjunct instructor. He explains:

> I concluded that getting this deep into lesson analysis with these
> students' first attempts at teaching might be "too much, too soon"
> and adjusted the assignment to allow them to select one of their
> four lesson plans to develop in lesson-study format and refine that
> lesson with the help of classmates prior to teaching. The lesson
> would then be videotaped and the student was to watch the vid-
> eotape and reflect on her or his own lesson in writing. In addition,
> I would ask them a few probing but relatively benign questions
> immediately following their lesson to help them process the teach-
> ing of the lesson. Five classmates provided written feedback to the
> student in each video after viewing the lesson. I provided a half

sheet of paper with two columns, one labeled "warm feedback" and the other labeled "cool feedback." After the forms were completed, I gave them a quick glance before passing the comments along to the student who presented the lesson. I noticed that, for the most part, the comments were positive; however, there were a few cool comments that most likely would not have been made if done in a class-wide forum.

The students' written reflections on their own lessons provided me with insight into the value of this activity. Although there were the typical statements, such as, "I was pleased with the lesson I presented," or "My lesson was not perfect," I was surprised by other statements, such as, "Teaching the lesson was exhilarating to me," "I was able to observe the person in the video in a detached manner," and, "I don't feel like quitting, which is most definitely the way I felt after teaching my first lesson."

Nevertheless, the purpose of the postconference in lesson study is to look deeply at the teaching process, and such comments are more personal than professional in nature. Comments that came closer to the purpose of lesson review included: "I wanted to focus on pulling out what information is given and what information is requested," "Students might have benefited more by modeling several break-even problems rather than one problem with multiple parts," "The bingo card analogy turned out to be an effective connection that the students used to relate to matrices," and "I believe I should develop leading questions for each ecosystems group." These comments indicate that the teachers were thinking critically about their teaching in a manner that would make their subsequent lessons better for their future students.

At the end of the semester I asked these students to answer a number of questions. The first had to do with the perceived value of the lesson-study process. One student responded, "I think that in life, ideas in isolation are limited." Another commented,

> Yes, I feel that cooperative planning can be very beneficial to the preservice teachers. When you think about all of the different experience levels and achievement levels contained within a classroom such as this, there is a great opportunity for the sharing of knowledge. In addition, within these groups some students may be very new to lesson planning, or may have never even put lesson planning into practice. By allowing peer influence, feedback, and support, the preservice teacher's ability and even self-confidence can be augmented.

Students also expressed opinions about the relative merits of different approaches to collaborative planning: "Realistically, I think that helping one another with individual lessons is more productive than actually planning a lesson collaboratively. It absolutely helps to give and get feedback about certain lessons that were individually planned beforehand. Getting different perspectives can always help in perfecting a lesson, or changing it completely, if need be."

A second question had to do with the types of feedback provided. Most had a preference for a particular type of feedback, yet appreciated a balance.

> Feedback on our teaching [lessons] from other class members was more beneficial than receiving comments [from the instructor] on my lesson plan. In a way, the comments I received on my teaching are actually comments on my lesson plans. Let's face it, we reflect on our own lessons each time we do them, only the first time you asked me to verbalize my thoughts, I thought the warm/cool feedback was more helpful than the personal reflection, because it told me what others saw, not just what I saw and thought. The drawback of personal reflection is that sometimes it is too painful to admit mistakes, and if nobody else says anything, then you wonder, "Did anyone else notice that mistake?" [For example] I thought the Food Web lesson was my best, but as it turned out, it really wasn't—my worksheet had problems, and I deferred to a classmate about what carnivores eat whom.

Another student wrote:

> The feedback from my peers helped me see the positives that I would not have noticed from being overly self-critical. The personal reflection was helpful for me to account for myself, both positive and negative. The reflection helped me to see where I needed to improve, but also to recognize moments that went better than expected.

Several of the students noted that having a form helped to focus peers' responses: "I would like to have warm and cool feedback on forms, coupled with a discussion of how to improve the lesson with my classmates. I didn't receive any constructive criticism from my classmates on my first lesson when the forms weren't used. I think it was a missed opportunity."

Jim's analysis of his first foray into lesson study was as follows:

> Teacher educators have to ask themselves, "Is the extra time that is necessary to implement this process worth the result?" I have doubts about my first attempt at lesson-study framework in methods class but, after some refinement, I believe it will be worth the extra time. If lesson study is truly to be the framework for the class, then it should be part of nearly every class. In my first attempt, the lesson-study process was more of a corollary to the class as opposed to the framework. The students, and sometimes the instructor, seemed to lose sight of the role that lesson study was to play within the class. The theme of the class was teaching for understanding. Not only could it exist within the lesson-study framework; in some respects I wonder how one could occur without the other.

TOWARD A FULLER UNDERSTANDING OF TEACHER EXPERTISE

Much of the writing on teacher expertise conceptualizes it along a continuum, from novice to expert, that is related to age and experience rather than determined by them (Bond, Smith, Baker, & Hattie, 2000). It is well within the realm of possibility for an older and vastly experienced teacher to march in place at the novice level (i.e., the ineffective veteran) or, conversely, for a novice to sprint forward to the expert level (i.e., the "natural" teacher). In general, however, it is the case that time and experience matter, and, for most teachers, effectiveness increases considerably after the first few years (Kain & Singleton, 1996). Research with preservice teachers suggests that initially they tend to be preoccupied with their personal ability to fulfill the teacher role (Dreyfus & Dreyfus, 1986; Fuller & Bown, 1975), find it difficult to reason beyond immediate context, fail to make the connection between content knowledge and pedagogical knowledge (Penso & Shoham, 2003), and need practice in identifying and planning specific pedagogical goals that can improve teaching performance (Coulon & Lorenzo, 2002). Yet at every level of experience, it is possible for teachers to fail to learn from their mistakes.

There is a useful distinction between acceptable performance and genuine expertise, just as there is a difference between merely passing a course versus earning a letter grade of A. In our view, an "ordinary" teacher can be effective, but only an extraordinary teacher can qualify as an expert. Expert teachers learn to accept that teaching is a perpetually challenging profession that demands lifelong striving to become a more effective, just, responsive, and caring educator. Neither time nor experience alone is sufficient to sustain this effort; it requires expertise.

Expertise is a developmental process consisting of five elements:

1. Metacognitive skills
2. Learning skills
3. Thinking skills
4. Knowledge
5. Motivation (Sternberg, 2001)

Motivation is viewed as the driving force that sparks metacognitive skills, which then activate learning and thinking skills (Sternberg, 2001). These skills then provide feedback to the metacognitive skills, which lead to increased levels of expertise. A synthesis of the literature suggests that seven assertions, as summarized in Figure 5.3, can be made about the process of acquiring teacher expertise.

Expert teachers construct their understandings of pedagogy (Fosnot, 1989). This process begins as teachers analyze their own learning, discuss it with other teachers at various levels of expertise, and use reflective journals to document their insights. Contrary to the routine practices of teacher preparation institutions, however, construction of pedagogy can-

---

Figure 5.3 Research-Based Assertions About Expertise

1. Expertise occurs at the intersection of talent, experience, practice, and reflection.

2. The process of acquiring expertise is gradual, ongoing, and directed toward higher levels of skill.

3. Attaining high levels of expertise is dependent upon extensive experience and cumulative, deliberate practice that is self-monitored.

4. As expertise develops, professionals are better able to integrate their skills into a cohesive and ever-expanding repertoire.

5. Experts may not always solve a problem more quickly. They do, however, bring richer and more personal sources of information to bear on the problem that they are trying to solve.

6. Expertise is recognized by other experts and the culture as indicative of mastery and excellence in one or more domains.

7. Experts are capable of doing the right thing at the right time and reliably do so.

Sources: Berliner, 1994; Chi, Glaser, & Farr, 1988; Dörner & Schölkopf, 1991; Ericsson & Hoffman, 2003; Simon & Chase, 1973; Sternberg, 2001

not stop there. The next important task is to make explicit the connection between how children learn and how teachers teach (Duckworth, 1996; Rainer & Matthews, 2002). This can be accomplished when teachers analyze children's thinking by engaging in such activities as observing and interviewing children and collecting and analyzing examples of children's work, all with an eye toward construction of pedagogy (Fosnot, 2003). This is precisely what transpires in collaborative planning.

Although most studies of pedagogical expertise are small-scale and nonexperimental, it is possible to make the following research-based statements about teaching expertise (Berliner, 1994):

- An effective combination for teacher preparation consists of a strong knowledge base in content coupled with pedagogical skills (Stough & Palmer, 2003; Stronge, 2002).
- Acquiring more domain-specific knowledge is necessary but not sufficient; expert teachers organize and apply that knowledge in more meaningful ways (Bond et al., 2000).
- Knowing, learning, and settings are interrelated. In order to understand teacher learning, it is important to take this situated perspective (Putnam & Borko, 2000). The same teacher who is regarded by colleagues as a firebrand and troublemaker in one setting, well could be celebrated as an innovator and contributor in another (Clandinin & Connelly, 1996).
- As educators move in the direction of greater expertise, they develop automaticity for the repetitive operations that are needed to accomplish goals, are more sensitive to task demands and the social situation when solving problems, and are more opportunistic and flexible in their teaching (Berliner, 1994).
- The connection between teacher expertise and student achievement is not a simple cause and effect. One reason that studies of expertise do not rely on correlating student achievement with teaching practices is that there are many factors that affect student achievement that are unrelated to teacher performance (Bond et al., 2000).
- Research suggests that several activities are associated with higher levels of teacher expertise: working with other teachers, linking content knowledge with pedagogical knowledge, concentrating on a few specific tasks that would improve the lesson, directly observing teaching performance, and using a teach-reteach format (Ball, 2000; Calderhead, 1987; Coulon & Lorenzo, 2002, Panasuk & Sullivan, 1998; Penso & Shoham, 2003; Wideen, Mayer-Smith, & Moon, 1998).

Unless and until professional growth is understood and experienced as a continuum of adult development, the teaching force will not improve significantly, and efforts to increase student achievement will fall short of the mark. Public schools in the United States cannot afford to treat the existence of master teachers as a happy accident. Just as the mentoring of new teachers should not be left to chance, there is an equal obligation to support the professional development of experienced educators as well as to change the way that preservice teachers are prepared, all with an eye toward responsible colleagueship. The trajectory of professional development for educators may be conceptualized as progressing from declarative knowledge (learning about teaching), to procedural knowledge (situated, can-do rudiments of pedagogy), to stable procedural knowledge (the basics of effective instruction), to expert, adaptive knowledge (the ability to adjust teaching to individual learners), and finally to reflective, organized, and analyzed knowledge (the capacity to function as a consultant teacher with colleagues) (Snow, Griffin, & Burns, 2005). If society continues to ignore that teachers at all levels require comprehensive, systematic, ongoing support in order to fully realize their potential as educators of the young, it is a great disservice not only to educators but also to children.

CONCLUSION: IN PURSUIT OF TEACHER WISDOM

The California Department of Education (2001) has defined excellence in teaching in terms of six teaching performance expectations. Excellent teachers are adept at

1. Creating and maintaining an effective environment for students
2. Understanding and organizing subject-matter knowledge for student learning (making subject matter comprehensible to students)
3. Planning instruction and designing learning experiences for all students
4. Engaging and supporting all students in learning
5. Assessing student learning
6. Developing as a professional educator

Such standards reflect the philosophy that preparation of teachers is a process that does not end with the completion of a teacher preparation program; rather, it leads to wisdom. As Sternberg (2004) argues, wisdom is, first and foremost, focused on the common good. It considers interests (intrapersonal, interpersonal, and extrapersonal) in order to achieve a balance over time (short-term and long-term) among responses to environmental contexts (adapting and shaping existing contexts, selecting new ones) as influenced by a system of values. We have adapted the three propositions of Sternberg's (2004) balance theory of wisdom to collaborative teacher planning as follows:

1. Teachers need creative abilities to generate ideas, and analytical abilities to decide whether their ideas (and those of others) are good ideas.
2. Teachers also need practical abilities to make ideas functional and to persuade other people of the value of their ideas.
3. Wisdom is what enables a teacher to consider and balance the effects of teachers' ideas not only on themselves but also on others and on institutions, both in the short and the long term.

Based on a 5-year study of the professional lives of literacy teachers, Judith Langer (2002) concluded that schools are more effective when they share the following six attributes:

- Professionalism is valued.
- Teachers have access to professional development resources.
- Teachers are encouraged to function as members of professional communities.
- Teachers participate in meaningful decision-making processes.
- Teachers care about the curriculum and student learning.
- Teachers make the commitment to become lifelong learners. (p. 1)

The last great outgrowth of a professional career as a teacher is expertise supported by wisdom. Collaborative planning processes are a major way of cultivating that expertise, capitalizing on teachers' collective wisdom of practice, and teaching to a higher standard.

Web Sources for Lesson Design, Planning, and Teacher Networks

Qiuyun Lin, Larry Tinnerman, and Mary Renck Jalongo

A to Z Teacher Stuff: http://www.atozteacherstuff.com
Created by teachers, the site features teacher discussion forums, lesson plans, themes, teaching tips, and other resources.

Becoming a Teacher: www.teachernet.com/htm/becomingateacher.htm
Designed for novices, this site is designed to support teachers as they strive to fulfill the teaching role.

Collaborative Lesson Plan Book (CLPB): http://web.utk.edu/~lre4life/ftp/clpb-samp.doc
This online document recommends a lesson-plan book designed by Tennessee teachers and administrators for their LIFE Project, ideal for use by an instructional team during weekly planning meetings. It also includes templates for designing a differentiated and individualized lesson plan.

Cool Teaching Lessons and Units: http://www.coollessons.org/coolunits.htm
This site provides links to ready-made units and lessons for all subjects as well as resources for lesson design, such as webquests, research models, and problem-based learning. Numerous links to other sites also are provided.

Designing a Lesson: http://www.rmcdenver.com/useguide/lessons/design.htm
This site features ideas, activities, and promising practices that support teachers in the process of lesson design. The site includes suggestions of ways to get started, sample plans and resources, design tips from experts, and other useful information.

Differentiated Instruction Lesson Plan: http://www.schoolhousedoor.com/teacher/experts-craig-diffinstr.htm
In this site, Dr. Susan Craig created a room for teachers to practice writing lesson plans that address differentiated instruction. Tools for making such a lesson plan (including a sample) are available.

Education Helper: www.edhelper.com
> This site contains thousands of worksheets, over 10,000 searchable lesson plans, thousands of WebQuests, educational programs, and spelling and vocabulary tools.

Education World: http://www.education-world.com/a_lesson
> This site provides lesson-planning help relating to curriculum topics. You can do a search or browse by topic on this site, which claims to provide 500,000 web resources.

How to Plan for Differentiated Instruction: http://www.teachnology.com/tutorials/teaching/differentiate/planning/
> This is an online tutorial that coaches teachers in ways to write lesson plans capable of addressing the needs of diverse groups of learners.

ikeepbookmarks: http://www.ikeepbookmarks.com
> This is an area where teachers store bookmarked sites online. An example of one school's bookmarks page is found at: http://www.ikeepbookmarks.com/gccs_lions. After teachers join, they can review the public bookmarks that other schools have selected.

Lesson Plan Design: http://www.su.edu/faculty/jcombs/lesson%20plans/comless.htm
> In a site designed for the initial teacher licensure program at Shenandoah University, a professor offers insights into lesson design and planning processes, including potential pitfalls and how to avoid them.

Lesson Planning: http://www.proteacher.com/020001.shtml
> Focusing on preK–8, ProTeacher takes you through the processes and components of lesson planning, step by step. You can create your own account, visit a community of elementary school teachers, and search for a growing collection of tens of thousands of ideas by teachers from across the United States and around the world.

Lesson-Planning Ideas: http://teacher.scholastic.com/lessonplans/
> Each school year, scholastic.com follows five outstanding classroom teachers. The lesson-plan ideas of these teachers, as well as a large collection of other sample lesson plans, can be browsed by grade level and content area at this site.

Lesson Plans and Instructional Resources: www.thegateway.org
> This website is a consortium effort to provide educators with quick and easy access to thousands of educational resources found on various federal, state, university, nonprofit, and commercial Internet sites.

Lesson Plans Page: http://www.lessonplanspage.com/index.html
> There are over 2,000 lesson plans stored on this site. The quality is mixed, but the collection can be used as a source of ideas for adapting to your own students. There are useful links to related sites, for example, how to plan a lesson, improving reading, science projects.

Lesson Research: http://www.lessonresearch.net
> In Japan, teachers improve their teaching through "lesson study," a process in

which teachers jointly plan, observe, analyze, and refine actual classroom lessons called "research lessons." This site provides background on lesson study and efforts to implement it in the United States.

Lesson Study: http://www.tc.columbia.edu/lessonstudy/
Lesson study is a professional development process that Japanese teachers engage in to systematically examine their practice, with the goal of becoming more effective. This site provides insights into the practice of lesson study, and guidance for teachers seeking to implement the practice in their schools. Many excellent resources are included in the Lesson Study Research Project Fall 2002 Reflective Report produced by the University of California, Los Angeles, and Ranch Bernard High School under the direction of Celeste Campbell.

Microsoft Lesson Connection: http://www.microsoft.com/education/LessonPlans.aspx
This program consists of two websites that allow educators to find lesson plans that fit 39 state standards.

Primary School Science: http://www.primaryschoolscience.com/about/about.php
Featuring a complete interactive lesson planning tool, this site offers a huge quantity of teaching materials, ideas, and resources to meet the requirements of the national guidelines. The site's purpose is to make the process of planning science lessons more efficient for teachers.

Project-Based Learning: http://pblchecklist.4teachers.org
This site is intended to assist teachers in evaluating the outcomes of collaborative learning projects. It supports teachers in creating custom checklists to suit their own and their students' needs by choosing from the options provided. The checklists produce set criteria and evaluate various aspects of students' work, such as oral presentations, class newspaper, reports, a puppet show, and so forth.

Sites for Teachers: www.sitesforteachers.com
This site contains a collection of links to nearly 900 education sites, rated by popularity, for teachers, parents, and students in K–12 schools.

Tapped In: http://tappedin.org/tappedin/do/LoginAction?state=promptGuest Login
Tapped In is a web-based learning environment created by SRI International to transform teacher professional development. The site's purpose is to offer high-quality, low-cost, online professional development experiences. Educators have Internet access to online tools, resources, colleagues, and support as they strive to implement effective, classroom-centered learning activities.

Teacher Planet: http://www.teacherplanet.com
This site features over 150 theme-based resource pages listed both alphabetically and chronologically. Also included are lesson plans, worksheets, free software, teacher tools, and so on. This site is particularly suitable for teachers planning a lesson on social studies.

Teachers' Internet Use Guide: http://rmcdenver.com/useguide
>   This site supports educators in designing, developing, implementing, and
>   evaluating an Internet-based lesson using a four-step instructional design
>   process. Sample lessons illustrate this process. The site includes an online
>   bank of teacher-created lessons.

Teaching Tips: http://honolulu.hawaii.edu/intranet/committees/FacDevCom/
guidebk/teachtip/teachtip.htm
>   This site offers a vast assortment of links covering topics in preparing a les-
>   son plan, course design, teaching techniques, assessment techniques, using
>   questions effectively, understanding how people learn, developing students'
>   core abilities, motivating students to learn, coping with stress, and guiding
>   student behavior.

The Teacher's Corner: http://www.theteacherscorner.net
>   Geared toward elementary and intermediate teachers, this site collects hun-
>   dreds of lesson plans, thematic units, and teacher resource pages.

Urban Education Exchange: http://www.haemimont.com/solutions_elearning.
php
>   This is a commercial site that functions to help teachers create lesson plans
>   and curriculum materials, organize and manage resources for their classes,
>   keep track of student data, manage courses online, design lessons and tests,
>   and create an online grade book.

Useful Websites for Educators: http://www.utea.org/links/nealinks/pro_dev-
Links.htm
>   Sponsored by the Utah Education Association, this site consists of a collection
>   of web links for teachers focusing on professional development.

WebQuests: http://webquest.sdsu.edu/webquest.html
>   A WebQuest is "an inquiry-oriented activity in which most or all of the infor-
>   mation used by learners is drawn from the Web." The activities are carefully
>   structured and many examples are available. This is possibly the most used
>   model worldwide for designing web-based lessons. Full guidance is avail-
>   able.

References

Abbott, L. (2003). Novice teachers' experiences with telementoring as learner-centered professional development. Retrieved March 31, 2006, from http://teach-net.edb.utexas.edu/%7Elynda_abbott/Researchfocus.html

Adams, J. E. (2000a). *A new way of thinking: Beginning teacher coaching through Garmston's and Costa's states of mind.* Palo Alto, CA: Palo Alto Unified School District.

Adams, J. E. (2000b). *Taking charge of curriculum: Teacher networks and curriculum implementation.* New York: Teachers College Press.

Ajzen, I., & Fishbein, M. (1980). *Understanding attitudes and predicting social behaviour.* Englewood Cliffs, NJ: Prentice Hall.

Arbuckle, M. (2000). Triangle of design, circle of culture. In P. Senge (Ed.), *Schools that learn: A fifth discipline fieldbook for educators, parents, and everyone who cares about education* (pp. 325–338). New York: Doubleday.

Ashby, R., Lee, P. J., & Shemilt, D. (2005). Putting principles into practice: Teaching and planning. In M. S. Donovan & J. D. Bransford (Eds.), *How students learn: History, mathematics, and science in the classroom* (pp. 79–178). Washington, DC: National Academies Press.

Ayers, W. (2001). *To teach: The journey of a teacher* (2nd ed.). New York: Teachers College Press.

Ball, D. L. (2000). Bridging practices: Intertwining content and pedagogy in learning to teach. *Journal of Teacher Education, 51*(3), 241–247.

Ball, D., & Cohen, D. (1999). Developing practice, developing practitioners: Toward a theory of professional education. In G. Sykes & L. Darling-Hammond (Eds.), *Teaching as the learning profession: Handbook of policy and* practice (pp. 3–32). San Francisco: Jossey-Bass.

Belenky, M. F., Clinchy, B. M., Goldberger, N. R., & Tarule, J. M. (1997). *Women's ways of knowing: The development of self, voice, and mind* (10th anniversary ed.). New York: Basic Books.

Berliner, D. C. (1994). Expertise: The wonder of exemplary performances. In J. N. Mangiere & C. C. Block (Eds.)., *Creating powerful thinkers in teachers and students* (pp. 161–186). Orlando, FL: Holt, Rinehart & Winston.

Bischoff, P. J., Hatch, D. D., & Watford, L. J. (1999). The state of readiness of initial level preservice middle grades science and mathematics teachers and its implications on teacher education programs. *School Science and Mathematics, 99*(7), 394–399.

Block, C. C., & Pressley, M. (Eds.). (2001). *Comprehension instruction: Research-based best practices.* New York: Guilford.

Bond, L., Smith, T., Baker, W. K., & Hattie, J. A. (2000). *The certification system of the National Board for Professional Teaching Standards: A construct and consequential validity study.* Greensboro, NC: Center for Educational Research and Evaluation.

Borko, H., & Livingston, C. (1989). Cognition and improvisation: Differences in mathematics instruction by expert and novice teachers. *American Educational Research Journal, 26*(4), 473–498.

Bredekamp, S., & Rosegrant, T. (Eds.). (1992). *Reaching potentials: Appropriate curriculum and assessment for young children* (Vol. 1). Washington, DC: National Association for the Education of Young Children.

Broudy, H. S. (1977). Types of knowledge and purposes of education. In R. C. Anderson, R. J. Spiro, & W. E. Montague (Eds.), *Schooling and the acquisition of knowledge* (pp. 1–17). Hillsdale, NJ: Erlbaum.

Bruner, J. (1997). *The culture of education.* Boston: Harvard University Press.

Bullough, R. V., & Gitlin, A. D. (2001). *Becoming a student of teaching: Linking knowledge production and practice* (2nd ed.). New York: RoutledgeFalmer.

Burnaford, G., Fischer, J., & Hobson, D. (Eds.). (2001). *Teachers doing research: The power of action through inquiry* (2nd ed.).Mahwah, NJ: Erlbaum.

Butler, D. L., Lauscher, H. N., Jarvis-Selinger, S., & Beckingham, B. (2004). Collaboration and self-regulation in teachers' professional development. *Teaching and Teacher Education, 20*(5), 435–455.

Cady, J. M. (1998). Reflective practice groups in teacher induction: Building professional community via experiential knowledge. *Education, 113*(3), 459–471.

Calderhead, J. (1984). *Teachers' classroom decision making.* London: Holt, Reinhart, & Winston.

Calderhead, J. (Ed.). (1987). *Exploring teachers' thinking.* London: Cassell.

California Department of Education. (2001). *California standards for the teaching profession.* Sacramento: Author.

Callahan, R. S. (1964). *Education and the cult of efficiency.* Chicago: University of Chicago Press.

Cambone, J. (1995). Time for teachers in school restructuring. *Teachers College Record, 96*(3), 512–543.

Campbell, C. (2002). *Lesson study research project.* Available at http://www.tc.columbia.edu/lessonstudy/worksharing.html

Campoy, R. W. (2000). *A professional development school partnership: Conflict and collaboration.* Westport, CT: Bergin & Garvey.

Carlgren, I. (1999). Professionalism and teachers as designers. *Journal of Curriculum Studies, 31*(1), 43–56.

Chapman, L. H. (2004). No child left behind in art? *Arts Education Policy Review, 106*(2), 3–17.

Chi, M. T. H., Glaser, R., & Farr, M. J. (Eds.). (1988). *The nature of expertise.* Hillsdale, NJ: Erlbaum.

Chokshi, S., & Fernandez, C. (2004). Challenges to importing Japanese lesson study: Concerns, misconceptions, and nuances. *Phi Delta Kappan, 85*(7), 520–525.

Christensen, L. (2002). *Reading, writing and rising up: Teaching about social justice and the power of the written word.* Milwaukee, WI: Rethinking Schools.

Clandinin, D. J., & Connelly, F. M. (1996). Teachers' professional knowledge landscapes: Teacher stories—stories of teachers—school stories—stories of schools. *Educational Researcher, 25*, 24–30.

Clark, C. M. (1983). Research on teacher planning: An inventory of the knowledge base. In D. C. Smith (Ed.), *Essential knowledge for beginning teachers.* Washington, DC: American Association of Colleges for Teacher Education.

Clark, C. M. (1996). *Thoughtful teaching.* New York: Teachers College Press.

Clark, C. M., & Peterson, P. (1986). Teachers' thought processes. In M. C. Wittrock (Ed.), *Handbook of research on teaching* (3rd ed.; pp. 255–296). New York: Macmillan.

Clark, C. M., & Yinger, R. J. (1979a). Teachers' thinking. In P. Peterson & H. J. Walberg (Eds.), *Research on teaching: Concepts, findings, and implications* (pp. 231–263). Berkeley, CA: McCutchan.

Clark, C. M., & Yinger, R. J. (1979b). *Three studies of teacher planning* (Research Series No. 55). East Lansing: Michigan State University, Institute for Research on Teaching.

Clark, C. M., & Yinger, R. J. (1987). Teacher planning. In J. Calderhead (Ed.), *Exploring teachers' thinking* (pp. 84–103). London: Cassell.

Cochran-Smith, M. (2004). *Walking the road: Race, diversity, and social justice in teacher education.* New York: Teachers College Press.

Cochran-Smith, M., & Lytle, S. L. (1993). *Inside/outside: Teacher research and knowledge.* New York: Teachers College Press

Cochran-Smith, M., & Lytle, S. L. (2002). Beyond certainty: Taking an inquiry stance on practice. In A. Literman & L. Miller (Eds.), *Teachers caught in the action: Professional development that matters* (pp. 45–60). New York: Teachers College Press.

Collinson, V., & Ono, Y. (2001). The professional development of teachers in the United States and Japan. *European Journal of Teacher Education, 24*(2), 223–248.

Cornbleth, C. (1987). The persistence of myth in teacher education and teaching. In T. S. Popkewitz (Ed.), *Critical studies in teacher education: Its folklore, theory and practice* (pp. 186–210). London: Falmer Press.

Costa, A., & Garmston, R. (1994). *Cognitive coaching: A foundation for renaissance schools.* Norwood, MA: Christopher-Gordon.

Coulon, S. C., & Lorenzo, D. C. (2002). The effects of supervisory task statements on preservice teachers' instructional behaviors during retaught lessons. *Education, 124*(1), 181–193.

Cunningham, J. W., & Creamer, K. H. (2003). Achieving best practices in literacy instruction. In L. B. Gambrell & L. M. Morrow (Eds.), *Best practices in literacy instruction* (2nd ed., pp. 333–346). New York: Guilford.

Curcio, F. R. (2002). *Japanese lesson study: Ideas for improving mathematics education* (user's guide, 34 pp.). Reston, VA: National Council of Teachers of Mathematics.

Danielson, C. (1996). *Enhancing professional practice: A framework for teaching*. Alexandria, VA: Association for Supervision and Curriculum Development.

Darling-Hammond, L. (1997). *The right to learn: A blueprint for creating schools that work*. San Francisco: Jossey-Bass.

Darling-Hammond, L. (2003a). Keeping good teachers: What leaders can do. *Educational Leadership, 60*(8), 6–13.

Darling-Hammond, L. (2003b). Teacher learning that supports student learning. In A. C. Ornstein, L. S. Behar-Horenstein, & E. F. Pajak (Eds.), *Contemporary issues in curriculum* (3rd ed.). Boston: Allyn & Bacon.

Darling-Hammond, L. (2006). *Powerful teacher education: Lessons from exemplary programs*. San Francisco: Jossey-Bass.

Darling-Hammond, L., & Bransford, J. (2005). *Preparing teachers for a changing world: What teachers should know and be able to do*. New York: Wiley.

Davenport, J., & Smetana, L. (2004). Helping new teachers achieve excellence. *The Delta Kappa Gamma Bulletin, 70*(2), 18.

Davies, D., & Rogers, M. (2000). Pre-service primary teachers' planning for science and technology activities: Influences and constraints. *Research in Science & Technological Education, 18*(2), 215–225.

Davis, B., & Sumara, D. J. (1997). Cognition, complexity, and teacher education. *Harvard Educational Review, 67*, 105–125.

De Jong, O. (2000). The teacher trainer as researcher: Exploring the initial pedagogical content concerns of prospective science teachers. *European Journal of Teacher Education, 23*(2), 127–137.

De Jong, O., Ahtee, M., Goodwin, A., Hatzinkita, V., & Koulaidis, V. (1999). An international study of prospective teachers' initial teaching conceptions and concerns: The case of teaching "combustion." *European Journal of Teacher Education, 22*(1), 45–59.

Dewey, J. (1910). *Influence of Darwin on philosophy and other essays*. New York: Henry Holt.

Dewey, J. (1933). *How we think*. New York: Heath.

Donovan, M. S., & Bransford, J. D. (Eds.). (2005). *How students learn: History, mathematics, and science in the classroom*. Washington, DC: National Academies Press.

Dörner, D., & Schölkopf, J. (1991). Controlling complex systems; or, Expertise as "grandmother's know-how." In K. A. Ericsson & J. Smith (Eds.), *Toward a general theory of expertise* (pp. 218–239). New York: Cambridge University Press.

Dorph, G. Z. (1997). Beyond prepared materials: Fostering teacher learning in the service of children's learning. *Religious Education, 92*(4), 459–478.

Dreyfus, H. L., & Dreyfus, S. E. (1986). *Mind over machine*. New York: Free Press.

Duckworth, E. (1996). *The having of wonderful ideas and other essays on teaching and learning* (2nd ed.). New York: Teachers College Press.

DuFour R., & Eaker, R. (1998). *Professional learning communities at work*. Bloomington, IN: National Educational Service.

Eaker, R., Dufour, R., & Burnett, R. (2002). *Getting started: Reculturing schools to become professional learning communities*. Bloomington, IN: National Educational Service.

Eby, J. W., Herrell, A. L., & Jordan, M. L. (2005). *Teaching K–12 schools: A reflective action approach* (4th ed.). Upper Saddle River, NJ: Prentice Hall/Pearson.

Egan, K. (1989). *Teaching as storytelling: An alternative approach to teaching a curriculum in the elementary school.* Chicago: University of Chicago Press.

English, F. W. (1992). *Deciding what to teach and test.* Newbury Park, CA: Corwin Press.

Ericsson, K. A., & Hoffman, R. R. (2003). Domain expertise. In J. W. Guthrie (Ed.), *Encyclopedia of education: Vol 2. Common-expertise* (2nd ed.; pp. 765–767). New York: Macmillan Reference USA.

Erikson, E. H. (1993). *Childhood and society* (Reissue ed.). New York: Norton.

Ershler, A. R. (2001). The narrative as an experience text: Writing themselves back in. In A. Lieberman & L. Miller (Eds.), *Teachers caught in the action: Professional development that matters* (pp. 159–173). New York: Teachers College Press.

Farley, F. (2001). A genetic model of creativity and the Type T personality complex with educational implications. In M. D. Lynch & C. R. Harris (Eds.), *Fostering creativity in children, K–8* (pp. 71–77). Needham Heights, MA: Allyn & Bacon.

Farstrup, A. E., & Samuels, S. J. (Eds.). (2002). *What research has to say about reading instruction.* Newark, DE: International Reading Association.

Feiman-Nemser, S. (2003). What new teachers need to learn. *Educational Leadership, 60*(8), 25–29.

Fenstermacher, G. (1994). The knower and the known: The nature of knowledge in research on teaching. In L. Darling-Hammond (Ed.), *Review of research in education* (Vol. 20; pp. 3–56). Washington, DC: American Educational Research Association.

Fenwick, T. J. (2004). Teacher learning and professional growth plans: Implementation of a provincial policy. *Journal of Curriculum and Supervision, 19*(3), 259–282.

Fernandez, C., Cannon, J., & Chokshi, S. (2003). A U.S.–Japan lesson study collaboration reveals critical lenses for examining practice. *Teaching and Teacher Education, 19*(2), 171–185

Fernandez, C., & Chokshi, S. (2002). A practical guide to translating lesson study for a U.S. setting. *Phi Delta Kappan, 84*(2), 128–134.

Feynman, R. (1997). *Surely you're joking, Mr. Feynman!: Adventures of a curious character.* New York: Norton.

Fisher, R. (2002). *Inside the literacy hour: Learning from classroom experiences.* London: RoutledgeFalmer.

Fosnot, C. T. (1989). *Enquiring teachers, enquiring learners: A constructivist approach for teaching.* New York: Teachers College Press.

Fosnot, C. T. (2003). Learning to teach, teaching to learn: The Center for Constructivist Teaching/teacher preparation project. *Teacher Education, 5*(2), 69–78.

Freedman, S. W. (2001). Teacher research and professional development: Purposeful planning or serendipity. In A. Lieberman & L. Miller (Eds.), *Teachers caught in the action: Professional development that matters* (pp. 188–208). New York: Teachers College Press.

Freiberg, J. H. (2002). Essential skills for new teachers. *Educational Leadership, 59*(6), 56–60.

Friedland, B. L., & Walz, L. M. (2003). Experiential learning in a rural university clinical setting: Developing teaming skills across three courses. *Rural Special Education Quarterly, 22*(3), 28–34.

Fullan, M., & Hargreaves, A. (1996). *What's worth fighting for in your school?* New York: Teachers College Press.

Fuller, F. F., & Bown, O. H. (1975). Becoming a teacher. In K. Ryan (Ed.), *Teacher education: The 47th yearbook of the NSSE, Part II* (pp. 25–52). Chicago: Rand McNally.

Gable, R. A., & Manning, M. L. (1999). Interdisciplinary teaming: Solutions to instructing heterogeneous groups of students. *Clearing House, 72*(3), 182–185.

Gagnon, G. W., Collay, M., Dunlap, D., & Enloe, W. (1998). *Learning circles: Creating conditions for professional development.* Thousand Oaks, CA: Corwin Press.

Garmston, R., & Dyer, J. (1999). *The art of cognitive coaching.* Highlands Ranch, CO: Center for Cognitive Coaching.

Glasser, W. H. (1990). The quality school. *Phi Delta Kappan, 71,* 425–435.

Goodlad, J. (1984). *A place called school: Prospects for the future.* New York: McGraw Hill.

Gose, M. D. (2004). Curriculum animation. *The Educational Forum, 69*(1), 53–64.

Greenwood, C. R., Tapia, Y., Abbott, M., & Walton, C. (2003). A building-based case study of evidence-based literacy practices: Implementation, reading behavior, and growth in reading fluency, K–4. *Journal of Special Education, 37*(2), 95–110.

Griffin, S. (2005). Fostering the development of whole-number sense: Teaching mathematics in the primary grades. In M. S. Donovan & J. D. Bransford (Eds.), *How students learn: History, mathematics, and science in the classroom* (pp. 257–308). Washington, DC: National Academies Press.

Hargreaves, A. (1994). *Changing teachers, changing times: Teachers' work and culture in the postmodern age.* London: Cassell.

Hiebert, J., Gallimore, R., & Stigler, J. W. (2002). A knowledge base for the teaching profession: What would it look like and how can we get one? *Educational Researcher, 31*(5), 3–15.

Hiebert, J., & Stigler, J. W. (2000). A proposal for improving classroom teaching: Lessons from the TIMSS video study. *The Elementary School Journal, 101*(1), 3–20.

Himley, M. (1991). *Shared territory: Understanding children's writing as works.* New York: Oxford University Press

Hord, S. M., Rutherford, W. L., Huling-Austin, L., & Hall, G. E. (1998). *Taking charge of change.* Austin, TX: Southwest Educational Development Laboratory.

Hunter, M. (1994). *Enhancing teaching.* New York: Macmillan.

Ingersoll, R. M. (2001). Teacher turnover and teacher shortages: An organizational analysis. *American Educational Research Journal, 38*(3), 499–534.

Isenberg, J. P., & Jalongo, M. R. (1997). *Teachers' stories: From personal narrative to professional insight.* San Francisco: Jossey-Bass.

Jackson, D. H. (2004). Nurturing future educators. *Delta Kappa Gamma Bulletin, 70*(2), 15–18.

Jacobs, H. H. (1997). *Mapping the big picture: Integrating curriculum & assessment K–12.* Alexandria, VA: Association for Supervision and Curriculum Development.

Jacobsen, D. A., Eggen, P., & Kauchak, D. (2006). *Methods of teaching: Promoting student learning in K–12 classrooms* (7th ed.). Upper Saddle River, NJ: Pearson Merrill Prentice Hall.

Jalongo, M. R. (2002). On behalf of children: "Fictions of teamwork" [editorial]. *Early Childhood Education Journal, 29*(4), 217–219.

Jalongo, M. R., & Isenberg, J. P. (2007). *Exploring your role: A practitioner's introduction to early childhood education* (3rd ed.). Upper Saddle River, NJ: Pearson Education. (Chapter 12 companion website PowerPoint® slides, http://www.prenhall/jalongo/)

Jinkins, D. (2001). Impact of the implementation of the teaching/learning cycle on teacher decision-making and emergent readers. *Reading Psychology, 22*(4), 267–288.

Johnson, B. (2003). Teacher collaboration: Good for some, not so good for others. *Educational Studies, 29*(4), 337–350.

Johnson, S. M. (2006). *Finders and keepers: Helping new teachers survive and thrive in our schools.* San Francisco: Jossey-Bass.

Johnson, S. M., & Kardos, S. M. (2002). Keeping new teachers in mind. *Educational Leadership, 56*(6), 12–16.

Joyce, B., & Calhoun, E. F. (1996). Beyond the textbook: A matter of instructional repertoire. *Educational Horizons, 74*(4), 163–168.

Joyce, B., & Showers, B. (1981). Transfer of training: The contribution of "coaching." *Journal of Education, 163*(2), 163–173.

Kagan, D. M., & Tippins, D. J. (1992). The evolution of functional lesson plans among twelve elementary and secondary student teachers. *The Elementary School Journal, 92*(4), 477–489.

Kain, J. F., & Singleton, K. (1996, May/June). Equality of educational opportunity revisited. *New England Economic Review,* pp. 87–111.

Kärräinen, M. (2000). Teams as network builders: Analysing contacts in Finnish elementary school teacher teams. *Scandinavian Journal of Educational Research, 44*(4), 371–391.

Kauchak, D., Eggen, P., & Carter, C. (2002). *Introduction to teaching: Becoming a professional.* Upper Saddle River, NJ: Merrill/Prentice Hall.

King, M. B., & Neumann, F. M. (2000).Will teacher learning advance school goals? *Phi Delta Kappan, 81*(8), 576–580.

Kostelnik, M. J. (Ed.). (1991). *Teaching young children using themes.* Glenview, IL: GoodYear.

Kraus, W. (1984). *Collaboration in organizations: Alternatives to hierarchy.* Dordrecht, The Netherlands: Kluwer Academic Publishers.

Langer, J. (2002). *Effective literacy instruction.* Urbana, IL: National Council of Teachers of English.

Lederman, N. G., & Niess, M. L. (2000). If you fail to plan, are you planning to fail? [Editorial]. *School Science & Mathematics, 100*(2), 57–60.

Leinhardt, G., & Greeno, J. G. (1986). The cognitive skill of teaching. *Journal of Educational Psychology, 78*(2),75–95.

LeTendre, G. (2002). Setting national standards: Educational reform, social change, and political conflict. In G. DeCoker (Ed.). *National standards and school reform in Japan and the United States* (pp. 19–32). New York: Teachers College Press.

Levande, D. (1988). *A descriptive study of teacher beliefs, teacher practices, and teacher-reported factors influencing reading instruction.* Unpublished doctoral dissertation, Columbia University Teachers College, Chicago. (Proquest Dissertation Abstracts, AAT 8824388)

Lewis, C. (2000, April). *Lesson study: The core of Japanese professional development.* Paper presented at the annual meeting of the American Educational Research Association, New Orleans. (ERIC Document Reproduction Service No. ED444972)

Lewis, C. (2002). *Lesson study: A handbook of teacher-led instructional change.* Philadelphia: Research for Better Schools.

Lieberman, A., & Grolnick, M. (1996). Networks and reform in American education. *Teachers College Record, 98,* 7–45.

Lieberman, A., & Miller, L. (Eds.). (2001). *Teachers caught in the action: Professional development that matters.* New York: Teachers College Press.

Linné, A. (2001a). The lesson as a pedagogic text: A case study of lesson designs. *Journal of Curriculum Studies, 33*(2), 129–156.

Linné, A. (2001b). Myths in teacher education and the use of history in teacher education research. *European Journal of Teacher Education, 24*(1), 35–45.

Litde, M. E., & Crawford, P. A. (2002). Collaboration among educators for true innovative programming. *Teacher Education and Special Education, 25*(3), 320–324.

Loucks-Horsely, S. (2000). Advancing technology education: The role of professional development. *The Technology Teacher, 60*(2), 31–34.

Ma, L. (1999). *Knowledge and teaching elementary mathematics.* Mahwah, NJ: Erlbaum.

Marzano, R. (2003). *What works in schools: Translating research into action.* Alexandria, VA: Association for Supervision and Curriculum Development.

Marzano, R. J., Pickering, D. J., & Pollock, J. E. (2001). *Classroom instruction that works.* Alexandria, VA: Association for Supervision and Curriculum Development.

Mastrini-McAteer, M. L. (1997). *Teacher beliefs and practices as they relate to reading instruction and student achievement.* Unpublished doctoral dissertation, University of Colorado at Denver Graduate School of Public Affairs. (Proquest Dissertation Abstracts AAT 9817730)

Maynes, B., Knight, D., McIntosh, G., & Umpleby, S. (1995). Lessons from exemplary practices of teacher evaluation. *The Canadian Administrator, 34,* 1–12.

McBride, M., & Skau, K. G. (1995). Trust, empowerment, and reflection: Essentials of supervision. *Journal of Curriculum and Supervision 10,* 262–277.

McCutcheon, G. (1980). How do elementary teachers plan? The nature of planning and influences on it. *Elementary School Journal, 81*(1), 4–23.

McCutcheon, G., & Milner, H. R. (2002). A contemporary study of teacher planning in a high school English class. *Teachers and Teaching: Theory and Practice, 8*(1), 81–94.

McEntee, G. H., Appleby, J., Dowd, J., Grant, J., Hole, S., & Silva, P. (2003). *At the heart of teaching: A guide to reflective practice.* New York: Teachers College Press.

McLaughlin, M. (1994). Strategic sites for teachers' professional development. In P. Grimmet & J. Neufield (Eds.), *Teacher development and the struggle for authenticity* (pp. 31–51). New York: Teachers College Press.

Meier, D. (2002). *In schools we trust: Creating communities of learning in an era of testing and standardization.* Boston: Beacon Press.

Meier, D. (2003). So what does it take to build a school for democracy? *Phi Delta Kappan, 85*(1), 15–21.

Metzger, M. (1993, June). Playing school or telling the truth? *Harvard Graduate School of Education Alumni Bulletin, 37*(3), 14–16.

Miller, L. (2001). School–university partnership as a venue for professional development. In A. Lieberman & L. Miller (Eds.), *Teachers caught in the action: Professional development that matters* (pp. 102–117). New York: Teachers College Press.

Miller, M. (2001). Assessing performance-based outcomes of multicultural lesson plans: A component within a comprehensive teacher education assessment design. *Multicultural Perspectives, 3*(1), 15–22.

Minnett, A. M. (2003). Collaboration and shared reflections in the classroom. *Teachers and Teaching: Theory and Practice, 9*(3), 279–285.

Mitchell, C., & Sackney, L. (2001, February 24). Building capacity for a learning community. *Canadian Journal of Educational Administration and Policy, 19.* Retrieved March 5, 2001, from http://www.umanitoba.ca/publications/cjeap/issues/19.html

Morris, M., Chrispeels, J., & Burke, P. (2003). The power of two: Linking external with internal teachers' professional development. *Phi Delta Kappan, 84*(10), 764–766.

Mosenthal, P. (1986). Research views: Defining good and poor reading–the problem of artifactual lamp posts. *The Reading Teacher, 39*(8), 858–861.

National Council for the Social Studies. (1994). *Expectations of excellence: National standards for social studies.* Washington, DC: Author.

Newfield, J. (1982). Teacher influence: A key concept for writing useful curriculum guides. *Education, 102*(4), 389–398.

O'Mahony, C. (2003). Facilitating child-focused planning in elementary social studies field placements. *The International Social Studies Forum, 3*(1), 255–259.

Onwu, G. O. M., & Mogari, D. (2004). Professional development for outcomes-based education curriculum implementation: The case of UNIVEMALASHI, South Africa. *Journal of Education for Teaching, 30*(2), 161–177.

Ornstein, A. C. (1997). How teachers plan lessons. *High School Journal, 80*(4), 227–237.

Panasuk, R., Stone, W., & Todd, F. (2002). Lesson planning strategy for effective mathematics teaching. *Education, 122*(4), 808–827.

Panasuk, R. M., & Sullivan, M. M. (1998). Need for lesson analysis in effective lesson planning. *Education, 118*(3), 330–334.

Parkay, F., & Stanford, B. H. (2001). *Becoming a teacher.* Boston: Allyn & Bacon.

Penso, S., & Shoham, E. (2003). Student teachers' reasoning while making pedagogical decisions. *European Journal of Teacher Education, 26*(3), 313–328.

Peter Harris Research Group. (2004). Supporting new teachers: The view from the principal's office. *School Administrator, 61*(10), 55–56.

Peter, J. D. (1994). The integration of research validated knowledge with practice: Lesson planning and the student history teacher. *Cambridge Journal of Education, 24*(1), 33–43.

Pierce, D., & Hunsaker, T. W. (1996). Professional development for the teacher, of the teacher, and by the teacher. *Education, 117*(1), 101–106.

Pinnegar, S. E. (1988, April). *Learning the language of practice from practicing teachers: An exploration into the term "with me."* Paper presented at the annual meeting of the American Educational Research Association, New Orleans.

Pong, W. Y. (2001, August 28–September 1). *Making conscious use of variation.* Paper presented at the Conference of the European Association for Research on Teaching and Learning (EARLI), Fribourg, Switzerland.

Poole, W. (1995). Reconstructing the teacher–administrator relationship to achieve systematic change. *Journal of School Leadership, 5,* 565–596.

Popkewitz, T. S. (1997). The production of reason and power: Curriculum history and intellectual traditions. *Journal of Curriculum Studies, 29*(2), 131–164.

Postman, N., & Weingartner, C. (1971). *Teaching as a subversive activity* (Reprint ed.). New York: Delta/Dell.

Power, B. M., & Hubbard, R. S. (1996). *Oops! What we learn when our teaching fails.* York, ME: Stenhouse.

Putnam, R., & Borko, H. (2000). What do new views of knowledge and thinking have to say about research on teacher learning? *Educational Researcher, 29*(1), 4–16.

Radford, D. L. (1998). Transferring theory into practice: A model for professional development for science education reform. *Journal of Research in Science Teaching, 35*(1), 73–88.

Rainer, J. D., & Matthews, M. W. (2002). Ownership of learning in teacher education. *Action in Teacher Education, 24*(1), 2–30.

Remillard, J. T. (1999). Curriculum materials in mathematics education reform: A framework for examining teachers' curriculum development. *Curriculum Inquiry, 29*(3), 315–342.

Remillard, J. T. (2000). Can curriculum materials support teachers' learning? *Elementary School Journal, 100*(4), 331–350.

Remillard, J. T., & Geist, P. (2002). Supporting teachers' professional learning through navigating openings in the curriculum. *Journal of Mathematics Teacher Education, 5*(1), 7–34.

Richhart, R. (2003). *Intellectual character: What it is, why it matters, and how to get it.* San Francisco: Jossey-Bass.

Routman, R. (1995). *Invitations: Changing as teachers and learners* (2nd ed.). Portsmouth, NH: Heinemann.

Rushton, S., & Larkin, E. (2001). Shaping the learning environment: Connecting developmentally appropriate practices to brain research. *Early Childhood Education Journal, 29*(1), 25–34.

Sardo-Brown, D. (1990). Experienced teachers' planning practices: A U.S. survey. *Journal of Education for Teaching, 16*(1), 57–71.

Schlechty, P. C. (1990). *Schools for the 21st century: Leadership imperatives for educational reform.* San Francisco: Jossey-Bass.

Schon, D. A. (1983). *The reflective practitioner: How professionals think in action.* New York: Basic Books.

Schon, D. A. (1987). *Educating the reflective practitioner.* San Francisco: Jossey-Bass.

Senge, P. (2000). *Schools that learn: A fifth discipline handbook for educators, parents, and everyone who cares about education.* New York: Doubleday.

Sennett, R. (1998). *The corrosion of character.* New York: Norton.

Sergiovanni, T. J. (1994). *Building community in schools.* San Francisco: Jossey Bass.

Shannon, P. (2000). We gotta get out of this place: The politics of what works. *The Reading Teacher, 53*(5), 394–396.

Shields, C. M. (2000). Learning from difference: Considerations for schools as communities, *Curriculum Inquiry, 30,* 275–294.

Shulman, L., & Sykes, G. (1986). *A national board for teaching? In search of a bold standard: A report for the task force on teaching as a profession.* New York: Carnegie Corporation.

Simon, H. A., & Chase, W. G. (1973). Skill in chess. *American Scientist, 61*(4), 394–403.

Sizer, T. R., & Sizer, N. F. (1999). *The students are watching.* Boston: Beacon Press.

Smith, C. (2003). Personal and professional development: Lessons from life. *English Leadership Quarterly, 25*(3), 2–4.

Snow, C., Griffin, P., & Burns, M. S. (2005). *Knowledge to support the teaching of reading: Preparing teachers for a changing world.* New York: Wiley.

Sternberg, R. J. (2001). Giftedness as developing expertise: A theory of the interface between high abilities and achieved excellence. *High Ability Studies, 12*(2), 159–178.

Sternberg, R. J. (2004). Wisdom and giftedness. In M. Ferrari & L. V. Shavinina (Eds.), *Beyond knowledge: Extracognitive aspects of developing high ability* (pp. 169–186). Mahwah, NJ: Erlbaum.

Stiff, L. V. (2000). Learning our lessons. *News Bulletin, 37*(4), 4.

Stigler, J. W., & Hiebert, J. (1999). *The teaching gap.* New York: Free Press.

Stigler, J. W., & Stevenson, W. (1991). How Asian teachers polish each lesson to perfection. *American Educator, 15*(1), 12–21, 43–47.

Stokes, L. (2001). Lessons from an inquiring school: Forms of inquiry and conditions for teacher learning. In A. Lieberman & L. Miller (Eds.), *Teachers caught in the action: Professional development that matters* (pp. 141–158). New York: Teachers College Press.

Stough, L. M., & Palmer, D. J. (2003). Special thinking in special settings: A qualitative study of expert special educators. *The Journal of Special Education, 36*(4), 206–222.

Stronge, J. H. (2002). *Qualities of effective teachers.* Alexandria, VA: Association for Supervision and Curriculum Development.

Sweeney, D. (2003). *Learning along the way: Professional development by and for teachers.* Portland, ME: Stenhouse.

Tann, S. (1993). Eliciting student teachers' personal theories. In J. Calderhead & P. Gates (Eds.), *Conceptualizing reflection in teacher development.* London: Falmer Press.

Taylor, N., & Vinjenold, P. (Eds.). (1999). *Getting learning right* (Report of the President's Education Initiative & Research Project Joint Educational Trust). Johannesburg, South Africa: JET Education Services.

Teitel, L. (2003). *The professional development schools handbook: Starting, sustaining, and assessing partnerships that improve student learning.* Thousand Oaks, CA: Corwin Press.

Tomlinson, C. A. (1999). *The differentiated classroom: Responding to the needs of all learners.* Alexandria, VA: Association for Supervision and Curriculum Development.

U.S. Department of Education. (1999). *Third international mathematics and science study.* Washington, DC: Author.

Vasquez, V. (2003). *Getting beyond "I like the book": Creating space for critical literacy in K–6 classrooms*. Newark, DE: International Reading Association.

Vaughn, S., & Linan-Thompson, S. (2004). *Research-based methods of reading instruction, K–3*. Alexandria, VA: Association for Supervision and Curriculum Development.

Wasley, P. (1999). Teaching worth celebrating. *Educational Leadership, 56*(8), 8–13.

Wassermann, S. (2004). *This teaching life: How I taught myself to teach*. New York: Teachers College Press.

Watanabe, T. (2002). Learning from Japanese lesson study. *Educational Leadership, 59*(6), 36–39.

Weeks, D. J. (2001). Creating happy memories. *Northwest Teacher, 2*(2), 6–11. (ERIC Document Reproduction Service No. EJ646411)

Westheimer, J., & Kahne, J. (2003). Reconnecting education to democracy: Democratic dialogues. *Phi Delta Kappan, 85*(1), 9–14.

Whelan, M. (2004). Back to basics, but that's just the beginning: Some reflections after observing an exemplary middle school unit. *The Social Studies, 95*(2), 53–61.

Whitbeck, D. A. (2000). Born to be a teacher: What am I doing in a college of education? *Research in Childhood Education, 15*(1), 129–136.

Wideen, M., Mayer-Smith, J., & Moon, B. (1998). A critical analysis of research on learning to teach: Making the case for ecological perspective on inquiry. *Review of Educational Research, 68*(2), 130–178.

Wiggins, G. (2003). "Get real!" Assessing for quantitative literacy. In B. L. Madison & L. A. Steen (Eds.), *Quantitative literacy: Why numeracy matters for schools and colleges*. Princeton, NJ: The National Council on Education and the Disciplines.

Wiggins, G., & McTighe, J. (1998). *Understanding by design*. Alexandria, VA: Association for Supervision and Curriculum Development.

Wilcox, B. L. (Ed.). (2002). Leadership and literacy. *English Leadership Quarterly, 25*(1), 3–4.

Wilms, W. W. (2003). Altering the structure and culture of American public schools. *Phi Delta Kappan, 84*(8), 606–615.

Wilson, S., & Wineburg, S. (1991, April). *Wrinkles in time and place: Using performance indicators to understand the knowledge of history teachers*. Paper presented at the annual meeting of the American Educational Research Association, Boston.

Wise, A., & Darling-Hammond, L. (1995). What is good teaching? *Teacher Magazine, 6*(8), 42–44.

Wood, K. (2000). The experience of learning to teach–Changing student teachers' ways of understanding teaching. *Journal of Curriculum Studies, 32*(1), 75–94.

Wood, K. (2003). Inside out and outside in—The role of variation in teachers' professional development. *Changing English, 10*(2), 205–213.

Yinger, R. J. (1980). A study of teacher planning. *Elementary School Journal, 80,* 107–127.

Yinger, R. J. (1987, April). *By the seat of your pants: An inquiry into improvisation and teaching*. Paper presented at the annual meeting of the American Educational Research Association, Washington, DC.

Yinger, R. J., & Nolan, A. L. (2003). Surviving the legitimacy challenge. *Phi Delta Kappan, 84*(5), 386–390.

Zeegers, M. (2000). Rhetoric, reality and the practicum: Reconstruction, behaviourism and primary teacher education in Papua New Guinea. *Asia-Pacific Journal of Teacher Education, 28*(2), 155–156.

Zeichner, K. M., & Liston, D. P. (1996). *Reflective teaching: An introduction.* Mahwah, NJ: Erlbaum.

Zemelman, S., Daniels, H., & Hyde, A. (1998). *Best practice: New standards for teaching and learning in America's schools.* Portsmouth, NH: Heinemann.

Index

About the Authors

Mary Renck Jalongo is a teacher, writer, and editor. As a classroom teacher, she taught preschool, first grade, and second grade; worked with children and families of migrant farm workers; and taught in the laboratory preschool at the University of Toledo. Currently she is a professor at Indiana University of Pennsylvania, where she earned the university-wide award for outstanding teaching and serves as the coordinator of a master's and doctoral program. As a writer, she has produced more than 20 books, many of them textbooks in the field of early childhood education. In addition, she has earned ten national awards for excellence in writing and teaching and has been the editor-in-chief of the Springer international publication, *Early Childhood Education Journal*, for 12 years.

Sue A. Rieg is currently an associate professor in the Professional Studies in Education Department at Indiana University of Pennsylvania, where she teaches education courses at the graduate and undergraduate levels. She served as an elementary school principal in the Indiana Area School District, where she also had been an elementary classroom teacher and instructional support teacher for almost 20 years. She has a doctoral degree in Administration and Leadership, a master's degree in Elementary Mathematics, and a bachelor's degree in Elementary Education. Research interests include pedagogy, assessment, and teacher stress factors.

Valeri R. Helterbran is currently an associate professor in the Professional Studies in Education Department at Indiana University of Pennsylvania, where she teaches both graduate and undergraduate students. Her background includes over 2 decades of experience in public schools—high school and middle school administration and secondary and elementary teaching. Her research interests include lifelong learning, professional development, and teacher professionalism.